The Occasions

Also by Eugenio Montale

Also by the translator, William Arrowsmith

TRANSLATIONS

The Bacchae; Cyclops; Orestes; Hecuba; and *Heracles* by Euripides
Satyricon by Petronius
Birds by Aristophanes
Clouds by Aristophanes
Dialogues with Leucò by Cesare Pavese
      (translated with D. S. Carne-Ross)
Alcestis by Euripides
Hard Labor by Cesare Pavese
That Bowling Alley on the Tiber by Michelangelo Antonioni
The Storm and Other Things by Eugenio Montale

EDITORSHIPS

The Craft and Context of Translation (edited with Roger Shattuck)
Image of Italy
Six Modern Italian Novellas
The Greek Tragedies in New Translations (in thirty-three volumes,
      in process of appearance)

The Occasions

Eugenio Montale

Translated, with preface and commentary, by
William Arrowsmith

W · W · Norton & Company
New York · London

Translation Copyright © 1987 by William Arrowsmith

Eugenio Montale, *Le Occasioni,* Copyright © 1957 Arnoldo Mondadori Editore; by arrangement with New Directions Publishing Corporation.

Claire de C. L. Huffman, *Montale and the Occasions of Poetry.* Copyright © 1983 by Princeton University Press.

Glauco Gambon, *Eugenio Montale's Poetry: A Dream in Reason's Presence.* Copyright © 1982 by Princeton University Press.

The Second Life of Art, Selected Essays on Eugenio Montale (edited and translated by Jonathan Galassi), translation copyright © 1982 by Jonathan Galassi. Published by the Ecco Press, 1982. Reprinted by permission of the Ecco Press.

Reprinted by permission of New York University Press from *Three Modern Poets: Saba, Ungaretti, Montale* by Joseph Cary. Copyright © 1969 by New York University.

Published simultaneously in Canada by Penguin Books Canada Ltd., 2801 John Street, Markham, Ontario L3R 1B4.
Printed in the United States of America.

The text of this book is composed in Bembo, with display type set in Bembo and Bembo Italic. Composition and manufacturing by The Maple-Vail Book Manufacturing Group.
Book design by Jacques Chazaud.

First Edition

Library of Congress Cataloging-in-Publication Data

Montale, Eugenio, 1896–
    The occasions.

    Translation of: Le occasioni.
    I. Arrowsmith, William, 1924–   . II. Title.
PQ4829.05650313   1987   851'.912   86–16269

ISBN 0-393-02316-8

ISBN 0-393-30324-1 (pbk)

W. W. Norton & Company, Inc., 500 Fifth Avenue, New York, N. Y. 10110
W. W. Norton & Company Ltd., 37 Great Russell Street, London WC1B 3NU

1 2 3 4 5 6 7 8 9 0

For I. B.

Contents

Translator's Preface

Montale's second book of poetry, *The Occasions,* was published in 1939, some fourteen years after the appearance of his celebrated first book, *Cuttlefish Bones.* Perceived as an act of courageous, if necessarily oblique, resistance to the Fascist regime, it won prompt critical approval. Discerning readers admired both its technical inventiveness and the poet's audacious effort to renew and contemporize the tradition of Dante and the other poets of the *Dolcestilnuovo* (the "sweet new style"). But its very intensity and concentration, as well as the privacy of much of the material and the poet's need to elude the censors by writing "between the lines," made it, at least for most readers, a book of formidable difficulty. Consequently, admiration for Montale's courage was mixed with complaints of obscurity, even obscurantism, and the book was relegated to that ill-defined and peculiarly Italian phenomenon known as "Hermetism." With this "movement"—little more than a reaction to Fascist bombast in the form of imperviously private verse—Montale's poetry has nothing in common except difficulty. At the time, however, the difference was not readily apparent, and, given the novelty of the poetic demands made by *The Occasions,* confusion was almost inevitable. Even now, nearly forty years later, those demands are arduous enough to daunt the most devoted readers.

Montale repeatedly, at times irritably, rejected the charge of obscurity. If his poems were difficult, he countered, they were certainly not so by design. Above all else he wanted to communicate. But his aim was the familiar modernist one of "making new," of creating the poetics apposite to a different human condition, a drastically altered reality. This, of course, entailed strenuous uphill work against inadequate or antiquated expressive modes, entrenched literary positions, and the aversion of readers to poetry that failed to satisfy traditional notions of the "poetic." To conventional readers, Montale's work, with its grainy avoidance of embellishment, freighted ellipses, and tonal intricacy, seemed crabbed, harsh, even antimusical. And the modernist poet's effort to make himself truly contemporary was, in the Italy of the thirties, complicated by the radical worsening of the political climate. Hermetic poetry, like private life generally, turned in on itself, away from the storm. Montale, instead of insulating himself, attempted to enclose the refractory contraries— public and private, external and internal, historical and individual, transcendental and immanent—within the confines of the poem. The result was poetry of a density and complexity almost unparalleled in Italian literature; a poetry that knowingly sought to make itself a *concentrate* of experience at the very instant when experience becomes most difficult and most intimidates expression.

This, it should be recognized from the outset, was Montale's avowed purpose: a poetry that risked making itself impossible or at best problematic. His work, he asserted, was "born of an intense concentration, and a confidence, perhaps excessive, in the material being treated." Neither romantic nor lyrical in the ordinary sense, the resulting poetry was unmistakably modern and modernist, an indigenously original Italian version of the *kind* of poetry—knotty, intricate, polysemous—championed elsewhere by Eliot, Apollinaire, and Valéry. In this respect, Montale's affinities with Eliot have often been noted (and, too often, exaggerated). Both, however, were genuine prosodic masters, just as both were committed to purifying "the language of the tribe" in order to do justice to the difficulty of contemporary reality. Both, in consequence, were charged with obscurity. In one crucial respect their poetics, though developed in isolation from each other and applied differently, were markedly similar. This was their view of the poem as an objectification of the feelings that "occasioned" it—what Eliot termed the "objective correlative." "On the most favorable hypothesis," Montale wrote just after the publication of *The Occasions,* "the so-called obscure poet is one who works on his own poem as though it were an object, accumulating in it instinctively sensory and supersensory things, there reconciling the irreconcilable, until he makes of it the firm and definite correlative of his own interior experience." Though diversely applied, it is this principle that makes the technical development of the two poets so strikingly parallel. Just as Eliot had sought, in the quatrains and the French poems, to curb the lyricism of "Prufrock" and "Portrait of a Lady," so Montale, to the dismay of admirers of *Cuttlefish Bones* (1929), had refused to repeat himself and slowly, poem by poem, worked out the taut, nervous, austere poetics of *The Occasions.*

Admittedly, intimations of this new poetics can be detected already in *Cuttlefish Bones*. Indeed, by deliberately adding a few poems from the decade of *The Occasions* to subsequent editions of the earlier book, Montale suggested a continuity. But the break with the previous style is nonetheless obvious. The lovely Ligurian land- and seascapes, the themes of lost innocence and precocious *senilità,* almost wholly disappear. The old lyrical voice is much harsher but also richer, with a new ironic complexity, pessimistically committed while faithfully despairing. The poet is now preoccupied with the individual's struggle to maintain psychic balance and human scale in a world veering out of control (see, for instance, "The Coastguard Station"). Tenderness for the vestiges of civilization and a great but vanishing tradition is everywhere manifest, as is the poet's effort, under increasingly adverse circumstances, to cope with the contradictions of his nature. If the book is less of a *canzoniere* than *Cuttlefish Bones*—everywhere linked by thematic and metaphorical, if not serial, continuity—it is nonetheless informed by the constant allusive presence of Dante and an (often ironic) Dantesque design: a (skeptical) poet's progress with its accompanying (elusive) vision, conversion, and (glancing) epiphany. The prosody is rigorously shaped to convey the stages of that progress; the harmonics faithfully "adhere" (Montale's word) to their emotional source. The aim is not statement but disclosure. Disclosure by what is *not* said; by the intimation, in both the poet and the world, of a void waiting to be filled. This void is disclosed by ellipsis and aposiopesis, by pointedly failed resolutions. The poems often trail away as though hinting at some marginal presence "beyond the frame" that might somehow, someday, fill them. Perfect cadence is refused, presumably in the hope of conjuring up a sense of what can only be hinted at, never seized. By being denied firm closure, the reader who craves it becomes involved in the predicament of the poem. He is forced to *feel time* by participating in *its* inability to achieve closure; moreover, he must experience time at just that instant when time seems to "mean" most powerfully and mysteriously. It was, I think, with this end in mind that Montale, by his own admission, adopted Gerard Manley Hopkins's "sprung rhythm." By so doing, he could escape the mindless *bel canto* confinement that so often afflicted Italian verse; he could confront his readers with the abruptness of tempo and tonal harshness that might jar them into startled attention, perhaps even receptivity, to the poem's temporal intimations.

   The Occasions, in short, began as a deliberate essay in "stylistic inhibition." To a degree, those inhibitions were, as we have seen, the reticence required of civilized poets by the Fascist regime. "My poetry in those days had no choice," Montale explained, "except to become more closed, more concentrated. (I don't say more obscure.)" But essentially the aim was a more expressive poetry capable of responding to the actual difficulty of the human situation, its frustrating *intermittences du coeur;* to complex juxtapositions of opposed or irreconcilable feelings; to the poet's sense of some mystery lying beyond the reach of language. What was needed was a new poetics, a different music:

> I obeyed a need for musical expression. I wanted my words to come closer than those of the other poets I had read. Closer to what? I seemed to be living under a bell-jar, and yet I felt I was close to something essential. A subtle veil, a thread, barely separated me from the definitive *quid.* Absolute expression would have meant breaking that veil, that thread: an explosion, the end of the illusion of the world as representation. But this remained an unreachable goal. And my wish to come close remained musical, instinctive, unprogrammatic. I wanted to wring the neck of our old aulic language, even at the risk of a countereloquence.

This, he observed, was the problem and the goal out of which *The Occasions* grew:

During this time I felt born in me the need for a stricter lyric poetry, more intensely *attaché a sa proie,* less explanatory. . . . I tried to live in Florence with the detachment of a foreigner, of a Browning; but I hadn't taken into account the henchmen of the feudal authority on which I depended [Montale was dismissed from his post as director of the Gabinetto Vieusseux in Florence for failing to join the Fascist party]. Besides, the bell-jar remained around me and now I knew it would never be shattered; and I feared that the dualism between lyric and commentary, between poetry and the preparation for or spur to poetry in my old experiments . . . remained heavily with me. I didn't think of pure lyric in the sense it later had in Italy too, of a play of suggestive sounds; but rather *of a product that would contain its sources without revealing them, or better, without stating them flat out. Granted that in art there is a balance between the occasion and the work or object, what was needeed was to express the object and conceal the occasion that gave rise to it.* A new means, not Parnassian, of immersing the reader *in medias res,* a total absorption of intentions in objective results. Here too I was moved by instinct, not theory. (Eliot's theory of the "objective correlative" didn't yet exist, I believe, when my "Arsenio" was published in *The Criterion.*) In substance, it doesn't seem to me that the new book [*The Occasions*] contradicted the results of the first; it eliminated some of its impurities and made an assault on that barrier between external and internal that seemed to me without foundation even from the epistemological viewpoint. For contemporary man everything is internal *and* everything is external, which doesn't mean that the world so-called is our representation. We live with an altered sense of time and space. . . .

This, in turn, led to a meditation on his transformation of the physical landscape of Liguria in *Cuttlefish Bones* into the more metaphysical landscapes of *The Occasions:*

In *Cuttlefish Bones* everything was attracted and absorbed by the fermenting sea; later on I saw that, for me, the sea was everywhere, and that even the classic architecture of the Tuscan hills was also movement and flight. And in the new book [*The Occasions*] too, I've continued my struggle to unearth another dimension in our weighty polysyllabic language, which seemed to me to reject an experience like mine. I repeat that the struggle wasn't programmatic. Maybe the unwelcome translating I was forced to do helped me. I've often cursed our language, but in it and through it I've come to recognize myself as incurably Italian: and without regret.

In sum, the unprogrammatic instinct to penetrate to the core of his own experience, to explore and re-create it, and, by so doing, objectify it, is the aim that animates *The Occasions.* Like Eliot and the cubist painters, the poet draws upon a tangled depth of "inner accumulation" which he seeks to concretize through meticulous suppression of decorative detail. The expression of this accumulation depends above all on what Montale called *musical voice*—an individual language that "becomes lyric through inner animation, not because it obeys the law of the metronome." A poet's voice is easily spoiled. Above all in a country like Italy where literary language—aulic and rhetorical, aristocratically disdainful of ordinary experience, and sustained by a powerful Mandarin tradition—has tended to produce mere virtuosity, poetry as *solfeggio* display. Timbre, the individual poet's personal capacity for registering tonal richness—overtone and undertone—can be ruined by vocal virtuosity, by inattention to what makes a given voice unique or by too facile a surrender to modish notions of musicality. Pedal is of course supremely important, the crowning musical achievement. A poet's voice may have astonishing timbre, he may be capable of richly expressive harmonic chords (like Montale's beautifully brocaded vowel sounds, intricate assonance, and off-rhymes). But if the pedal—that bass that is a significant stranger to the chords built above it—is missing, the poem is crippled, incomplete, deprived of true climax.

It is the absence of pedal in *The Occasions* of which Montale later complained in his own "Imaginary Interview." The book, he acknowledged, "was an orange, or rather a lemon, that was missing a slice; not really that of pure poetry . . . but of pedal, of deep music and contemplation." A lemon, not an orange: because the expected prosodic sweetness is missing; the music is harsh and acerb, the verse puckers in the mouth. Lacking a pedal, the orchestration is incomplete. Only with the publication of *Finisterre* (the opening section of *The Storm and Other Things* but also the thematic culmination of the "stylistic adventure" of *The Occasions*), would that missing slice, the pedal, be fully supplied. What was missing was the background of a warring world—"a war that is both cosmic and earthly, without an end and without a reason." But, at least in part, intermittent yet increasingly audible, the bass is repeatedly, darkly sounded. It is intimated in the ravaging storm of "Bellosguardo Times"; again, in the twilight world of "Boats on the Marne" as the river gathers for its fatal rush into the night and the unknowable ocean of the future; and in the apocalyptic "bad weather" of "News from Amiata." It is this ominous emergence of the pedal which gives *The Occasions* the urgency of dramatic climax. Moreover, the poet's struggle to locate a pedal suited to his individual voice, timbre, and thematic concerns is itself dramatic, a process of self-discovery, which has as its lexical counterpart the book's gradual revelation of the meaning of its own "occasions." Thus the poems of the first section are "occasional" verse because provoked by the events they objectify. But in the later poems these diverse objectifications begin to converge, "homing in" on *the* object, *the* occasion that was implicitly present in the earlier poems. In the course of the book, the technical quest for the poetics of the poem-as-object is transformed into the discovery of its real but unidentified quarry—Clizia, whose absence and/or presence provoked the quest in the first place. The poet-lover's passion, the void of his need, precedes the identification of the object that might satisfy it. In the quest the poet and the man—the lover—converge and are completed. Individual voice, timbre, pedal are all the consequence of a life-poetics. A poetics capable of signifying its true *religious* object—the "other," Clizia, the Muse—on the occasions of her miraculous appearance in the profane world.

The harmonics of the "object-occasion" are matched by a corresponding prosodic craftsmanship. The "poet-musician" (Montale's term for Eliot) is always, above all in his disdain for mere showman's virtuosity, in evidence. Not only in the dazzling metrical variety and mercurial shifting of tone between aulic and conversational, Tuscan and dialect, but in the overall musical structure, and the poet's uncanny skill of thematic variation and advance. The "key" is provided by the opening poem, "The Balcony," an image of the poet's darkened room, a domestic world lit only by the fitful radiance of sunlight to which the eyes of his Dantesque *donna*—his Beatrice, *donna pietrosa,* Delia, Laura, Mandetta, Selvaggia, Clizia—are wholly directed. In the final poem, "News from Amiata," the room from which the poet writes to his transhumanized *donna* has been cosmologized: "the honeycomb cell / of a globe launched into space"; the sunlight has become the brief flare of magnesium flashes from "the unseen peak" of a black-out world in universal bad weather. The light to which the *donna* directed her eyes is now contained by her "icon." *She* is the scrim through which the poet perceives the divine; it is her image that "reveals / the luminous background." His whole book, we now learn, is, like a *bouteille à mer,* a long, brokenly continuous, probably undeliverable love letter to Clizia, the poet's true *act* of *faith.* The transformation, the gradual limning of the emerging background, is enabled by the book's first section. Its dynamics are then applied to the book's centerpiece, the stunning sequence of the "Motets," and brought to fulfillment in the great poems of the final section, where the ultimate "object"—the epiphany of the absent Clizia—is revealed.

Montale's "poem-as-object" is, as I said earlier, strikingly like Eliot's "objective correlative": ". . . a set of objects, situations, a chain of events that shall be the formula of that *particular* emotion; such that when the external facts . . . are given, the emotion is immediately evoked." In Montale's practice the triggering occasion is an experience, emotion, or event, a quantum of mysterious energy in a situation, no matter how seemingly ordinary. In this "occasion" the poet detects potential significance, a "sign" pointing to full disclosure. The poem, by refusing direct statement or conventionally expressed "poetic emotion," discloses this "object." The given occasion may be, as in "Buffalo," an incandescent incident from a Parisian *vélodrome,* or, as in "Keepsake," a string of fortuitously linked "moments" from musical comedy, or the brief lightning flash of those Dantesque women or their *donne-schermo* (the various human scrims that compose and often conceal the dolcestilnovistic *donna*). But they are all, as poems, objectifications of the given stimulus-event. Of Dora Markus, one of the women who appear in these poems, Montale said that he never knew her; she was "constructed from a photograph of a pair of legs" sent him by a friend. However, the poem devoted to her is no mere exercise in virtuoso evocation; it is the objectification of the poet's affinity for a personalized truth, the existential meaning of a given fragment. "The poet's task," Montale observed, "is the quest for a particular, not general, truth. A truth of the poet-subject that doesn't deny that of the empirical man-subject. That sings what unites man with other men, but doesn't deny what separates him and makes him unique and unrepeatable."

With the "Motets," the book's great pivot-sequence and "objective correlative," the essential *donna* of Montale's poetry makes her appearance. Still fused with the *donne-schermo,* the "masked ladies" of the preceding section, it is she who, we now see, has been all the while looming in them, struggling to emerge from the mask. This ultimate *she* is Clizia, the Ovidian girl whose love for the god of light, Apollo, transformed her into a sunflower or heliotrope—that same sun-struck woman whose inspiriting presence is the subject of the prologue-poem, "The Balcony." As Montale always insisted against those who tried to reduce her to mere mistress status, "She is Dantesque, Dantesque!" Like Dante's Beatrice, she is both divine Muse and initiatrix; with her eyes, *through* her, *in* her, the poet glimpses, if not God, paradise and redemption. "Insofar as she [Beatrice] is a stylistic (or amorous) adventure (*aventura stilistica*)," Montale wrote, "she will never coincide with a real lady. But if Dante had a precocious intimation of Beatrice's ultimate significance (and the *Vita Nuova* leaves little doubt), I would say that both *donna Pietra* and the *donna gentile* [*donne-schermo* from Dante's earlier *Rime*] would have had to be invented out of thin air if they didn't exist, since it is impossible to imagine a process of salvation without the counterpart of error and sin." Full, comprehensive grasp of this judgment is, I believe, indispensable to understanding the role of Clizia in Montale's poetry and of the poetry itself.

In Italian *avventura stilistica* means not merely "stylistic adventure" but, more to the point, "stylistic love affair." The style in question is that of the *dolcestilnovisti,* the writers of the "sweet, new style," that circle of nympholetic poets of courtly love which included not only Dante but Cavalcanti, Cino da Pistoia, Guido Guinizelli, and, later, Petrarch. The cardinal tenet of their poetic faith was that Love, by the agency of the adored *donna,* ennobles the lover and may, at least in Dante's vision, conduct him even to God. In this dolcestilnovistic sense *The Occasions,* above all the "Motets" and the poems that trace Clizia's inspiriting presence-in-absence and miraculously saving interventions, can properly be called an *avventura stilistica.* The poet, saturated in tradition, attempts to resuscitate a mode of feeling so alien to modern erotic modes that the effort can only be viewed as an adventure verging on Quixotic audacity. But it is also an effort to revive an older form of feeling by means of a poetics that, like Eliot's, is based upon extremely adventurous musical and structural experimentation. *The Occasions* (and its coda, *Finisterre,* in *The Storm and Other Things*) is, in short, a book in which style is inseparable from the erotic epiphany at which it aims. You can't have the "adventure" unless you are prepared to accept the "style." And the boldness of the adventure is best grasped by recognizing the *fondo*—the cosmic setting—for which the book, in its quest for the pedal point, is plainly groping. As I suggested, *The Occasions* should be read as a visionary love affair that culminates in the startled discovery of Clizia, not merely as the absent center of the poet's life, but as the agent of his salvation—his and ours. The poetic and the human self are recognized through a transcendent "other"; by Clizia's sacrifice of physical love, she becomes her lover's spiritual salvation. Like Dante's Beatrice, she redeems not only her lover (even while he physically despairs), but all those who, like Montale, were suffering the darkness of the Fascist years and human evil generally. She "redeems the time." This, at least, was how the book was perceived by its more sensitive readers in 1939. To those trapped by physical or spiritual torpor, by political oppression or metaphysical limitation, she stands for the reality of freedom achieved, for the possibility of a passage to whatever higher world one aspires.

"Dantesque, Dantesque!" The originality of *The Occasions* needs, it seems to me, no argument or justification. No Italian poet of the twentieth century has taken greater experimental risks than Montale in this book, above all in the effort to renew the Dantesque vein in terms of a sensibility that belongs so passionately to its own time and strives so tenaciously to find an individual voice—a voice never to be repeated. In Montale's critical vocabulary there is no higher praise than that an artist's vision should be uniquely his own and therefore most universal; that he stubbornly and courageously refuse to repeat himself; that he should possess what Eliot called "the historical sense"—that sense of both timeless and temporal that makes a writer truly traditional and, at the same time, most aware of his own contemporaneity. It is in terms of these criteria that Montale's achievement should be recognized for what it is— a contemporary "poet's progress" consciously building upon the poetry of the past, but above all on the Dante of the *Vita Nuova*. That Montale recognized the affinity—that he was guided by Dante as Dante was guided by Virgil, and no less prepared to abandon his guide for that of his *donna*— there seems to me no doubt. "The *Vita Nuova*," Montale wrote, "gives a preliminary shape, already complete in itself, to what will become Beatrice's process of transhumanization. The story, which is better called a vision, also dwells on details that seem realistic today, but are intended to give form to the conflict between human spirits and transcendent vocation." Since Montale's own progress as man and poet is, like that of all mankind, a story of error and sin, it requires as its counterpart the "process of salvation" for which Clizia-Beatrice stands: beckoning, sternly exigent, a flesh-and-blood creature who has, by her own choice, become transcendent. About the process of transhumanization, Montale, like Dante, is silent. One knows what it is or one does not. For a *vision* there are no words:

> Trasumanar significa per verba
> non si poria; però, l'esemplo basti
> a cui esperienza grazia serba.

[Transhumanization may not be expressed in words; therefore let the example suffice any for whom grace reserves that experience.]

This translation represents my effort to render what I have understood of Montale's work: his poetics, thematics, and their fusion in a poem. Translating Montale is immensely rewarding; it is also, much of the time, very rough going; *crede experto!* The texture of the poetry is extremely complex; tonal shifts are often bewilderingly sudden; the suppression of transitions is dictated by an internal logic of feelings which is sometimes maddeningly elusive; the omnipresent ironies are intricately nuanced; the rhythms, suggestive of the constant to-and-fro of actual feeling, require a very delicate touch. Which is simply to say that translating Montale is frustratingly difficult; his translator is often left unhappily feeling that the meaning in the period or phrase he has translated may not be what Montale meant, or that he has translated only part of Montale's meaning, or even that he has missed the point altogether. But the frustration goes with the territory. If one translates a poet explicitly committed to expressing the inexpressible, he may have to settle for intuitive hunches.

In general, I have tried to translate according to a few rule-of-thumb principles derived from my sense of what accurate rendering of meaning and tone requires. I have therefore avoided prettification, embellishment, and traditional concinnities like the plague. Montale's "sprung rhythm" has been brought over with what I hoped was an analogously jarring abruptness; the constant dialogue between aulic and colloquial (Montale is emphatically not, as ignorant critics claim, "always conversational") has, insofar as possible in American English, been retained. I have conscientiously resisted the translator's temptation to fill in or otherwise modify Montale's constant ellipses, to accommodate *my* reader by providing smoother transitions. And I have done my best to honor Montale's reticence, his ironic qualifications, and evaded cadences. A chief aim has been to preserve the openness of the poet's Italian, even though this has meant resisting the genius of English for concreteness. (When the Italian text gives *ridere*, I have translated it as "laugh" rather than one of the more colorful modalities of laughter: chuckle, guffaw, titter, and so on.) Montale's syntax is formidable in its periodicity, rapidity, and transformational urgency: this, wherever possible—that is, within the bounds of credible English—I have endeavored to preserve. Above all, I have kept in mind that the ultimate aim of these poems is an *objectification* designed to evoke the difficulty and mystery of a life that precedes words, and that, even when the experience is evoked, survives them. To the translations themselves I have appended a body of notes that I hoped might prove useful to readers unfamiliar with Montale's work and its relation to Italian tradition and modern poetry generally. Where excellent commentary already existed, I have not hesitated to make use of it; where existing commentary was thin or critically inadequate, I have ventured to provide my own.

To Gertrude Hooker and Rosanna Warren, *le donne salutifere* of this enterprise, I owe much more than I can say for their meticulous, perceptive, and bracing criticism of most of these versions in their many successive drafts. Whatever merit they may have is due in large measure to their efforts to make me toe the Montalean line. Though we have never met, Jeffrey Gantz, acute and ardent *Montaliano,* with truly extraordinary generosity provided me with scrupulously detailed and very suggestive advice in fine-tuning both translations and notes. It is to this trio that this translation is enthusiastically dedicated.

Appreciative thanks for criticism of individual poems are owed to Stephen Berg, Stanley Burnshaw, Glauco Cambon, Ralph Chandler, Simone Di Piero, Jonathan Galassi, and Mark Rudman. Francesca Raggi, who typed the poems and helped me with many of the lexical and interpretative problems that confront the translator of Montale, has my deep gratitude. My editor at Norton, Kathleen Anderson, provided encouragement and, no less necessary, gently demanding deadlines. Norton's team of hawk-eyed copy editors, Nancy Palmquist and Leslie T. Sharpe, detected more errors than I thought possible, vetting the manuscript with rigor and sensitivity.

Boston, Mass. —William Arrowsmith

Il balcone

Pareva facile giuoco
mutare in nulla lo spazio
che m'era aperto, in un tedio
malcerto il certo tuo fuoco.

Ora a quel vuoto ho congiunto
ogni mio tardo motivo,
sull'arduo nulla si spunta
l'ansia di attenderti vivo.

La vita che dà barlumi
è quella che sola tu scorgi.
A lei ti sporgi da questa
finestra che non s'illumina.

The Balcony

It seemed child's play
to change the void yawning before me
into nothingness, your certain fire
into tedious uncertainty.

Now to that nothingness I have bound
my every sluggish motive,
that arduous void blunts my yearning
to serve you while I live.

You have no eyes for any life
but that shimmering you alone can see.
You lean out toward it
from this window, now unlit.

I

Vecchi versi

Ricordo la farfalla ch'era entrata
dai vetri schiusi nella sera fumida
su la costa raccolta, dilavata
dal trascorrere iroso delle spume.
Muoveva tutta l'aria del crepuscolo a un fioco
occiduo palpebrare della traccia
che divide acqua e terra; ed il punto atono
del faro che baluginava sulla
roccia del Tino, cerula, tre volte
si dilatò e si spense in un altro oro.

Mia madre stava accanto a me seduta
presso il tavolo ingombro dalle carte
da giuoco alzate a due per volta come
attendamenti nani pei soldati
dei nipoti sbandati già dal sonno.
Si schiodava dall'alto impetuoso
un nembo d'aria diaccia, diluviava
sul nido di Corniglia rugginoso.
Poi fu l'oscurità piena, e dal mare
un rombo basso e assiduo come un lungo
regolato concerto, ed il gonfiare
d'un pallore ondulante oltre la siepe
cimata dei pitòsfori. Nel breve
vano della mia stanza, ove la lampada
tremava dentro una ragnata fucsia,
penetrò la farfalla, al paralume
giunse e le conterie che l'avvolgevano
segnando i muri di riflessi ombrati
equali come fregi si sconvolsero
e sullo scialbo corse alle pareti
un fascio semovente di fili esili.

Era un insetto orribile dal becco
aguzzo, gli occhi avvolti come d'una
rossastra fotosfera, al dosso il teschio

Old Verses

I remember the moth that squirmed inside
the open windows in the steamy night
on the strip of coast awash
with the furious surges of the flung spray.
The whole twilit air quivered in a feeble
waning flicker of that thin line
dividing land from sea; and the faint tip
of the lighthouse flashed from the Tino cliff,
sky-blue, three times fanning out,
then subsided in a different gold.

My mother was sitting beside me
at a table cluttered with playing
cards propped two by two like
dwarf barracks for the toy soldiers
of grandchildren now dispersed to sleep.
Overhead a squall of icy air flailed
violently down, flooding over
Corniglia's rusty eyrie.
Then blackness, and from the sea
a deep bass roar insistent as a slow, restrained
adagio, and the swell
of a pallor undulating beyond the hedgerow
peaked with pittosporum. In the small
space of my room where the lamp
was blinking in a fuchsia web,
the moth worked its way inside, hit
the lampshade fringed with glass beads
marking the walls with shadowed reflections
like friezes wildly shaking,
and in the faint light there raced toward the wall
a self-propelled band of tiny beads.

It was a horrible bug, pointed
beak, eyes haloed as though
in a reddish photosphere, on its back a human

umano; e attorno dava se una mano
tentava di ghermirlo un acre sibilo
che agghiacciava.

Batté più volte sordo sulla tavola,
sui vetri ribatté chiusi dal vento,
e da sé ritrovò la via dell'aria,
si perse nelle tenebre. Dal porto
di Vernazza le luci erano a tratti
scancellate dal crescere dell'onde
invisibili al fondo della notte.

Poi tornò la farfalla dentro il nicchio
che chiudeva la lampada, discese
sui giornali del tavolo, scrollò
pazza aliando le carte—
                                          e fu per sempre
con le cose che chiudono in un giro
sicuro come il giorno, e la memoria
in sé le cresce, sole vive d'una
vita che disparì sotterra: insieme
coi volti familiari che oggi sperde
non più il sonno ma un'altra noia; accanto
ai muri antichi, ai lidi, alla tartana
che imbarcava
tronchi di pino a riva ad ogni mese,
al segno del torrente che discende
ancora al mare e la sua via si scava.

skull; and if a hand tried to seize it,
it filled the air with a savage hiss
that froze the blood.

It thumped dully once or twice on the table,
then thumped against the windows closed against the wind,
made its way outside on its own
and vanished in the darkness. Lights
from the harbor at Vernazza every now and then were
blotted out by the breakers heaving
invisibly in the black of night.

Then the moth came back inside the snail shell
enclosed by the lamp, fell
to the newspapers on the table, and, thrashing
frantically, sent the cards flying—
                                        and was forever one
with the things that close themselves in a secure
circle like the day, and memory makes them grow
inside itself, sole survivors of a single life
that vanished underground. And with them went
familiar faces dispersed no longer now
by sleep, but by another boredom: close
by the ancient walls, the beaches,
and the trawler that every month
shipped its cargo
of pine logs piled on the shore; close by the sign—
the torrent that still falls
seaward, carving its own way.

Buffalo

Un dolce inferno a raffiche addensava
nell'ansa risonante di megafoni
turbe d'ogni colore. Si vuotavano
a fiotti nella sera gli autocarri.
Vaporava fumosa una calura
sul golfo brulicante; in basso un arco
lucido figurava una corrente
e la folla era pronta al varco. Un negro
sonnecchiava in un fascio luminoso
che tagliava la tenebra; da un palco
attendevano donne ilari e molli
l'approdo d'una zattera. Mi dissi:
Buffalo!—e il nome agì.
                              Precipitavo
nel limbo dove assordano le voci
del sangue e i guizzi incendiano la vista
come lampi di specchi.
Udii gli schianti secchi, vidi attorno
curve schiene striate mulinanti
nella pista.

Buffalo

A sweet inferno, burst on burst,
in the loop of blaring megaphones, compacted
crowds of every color. Buses
spilled out, spurting into the night.
Heat steamed into smoke
over the swarming gulf; lower down an arc-
light formed a river
and the crowd was set to cross. A black man
lay dozing in a swath of light
slicing the darkness; in the stands
easy women were laughing, waiting for
a barge to land. I said to myself:
Buffalo!—and the spell worked.
                                    I plunged down
into that limbo where the voices of the blood
stun and glitterings burn away vision
like mirrors flashing. I heard
the dry cracks, all around I saw
bent striped backs pumping
down the track.

Keepsake

Fanfan ritorna vincitore; Molly
si vende all'asta: frigge un riflettore.
Surcouf percorre a grandi passi il cassero,
Gaspard conta denari nel suo buco.
Nel pomeriggio limpido è discesa
la neve, la Cicala torna al nido.
Fatinitza agonizza in una piega
di memoria, di Tonio resta un grido.
Falsi spagnoli giocano al castello
i Briganti; ma squilla in una tasca
la sveglia spaventosa.
Il Marchese del Grillo è rispedito
nella strada; infelice Zeffirino
torna commesso; s'alza lo Speziale
e i fulminanti sparano sull'impiantito.
I Moschettieri lasciano il convento,
Van Schlisch corre in arcioni, Takimini
si sventola, la Bambola è caricata.
(Imary torna nel suo appartamento.)
Larivaudière magnetico, Pitou
giacciono di traverso. Venerdì
sogna l'isole verdi e non danza più.

Keepsake

Fanfan's the winner; Molly auctions herself
off: a spotlight sputters.
With huge strides, Surcouf paces the poop;
Gaspard holes up and counts his cash.
On a cloudless afternoon the snow began
to fall, Cicala goes home to his nest.
Fatinitza agonizes in a fit
of amnesia; of Tonio a scream survives.
Fake Spaniards are dicing at the Brigands'
convent; but the dreadful
alarm clock goes off in a pocket.
The Marchese del Grillo is packed off
to the street; the wretched Zeffirino
turns clerk; the Pharmacist rises,
the matches strike on the tile floor.
The Musketeers abandon the convent,
Van Schlisch vaults to the saddle, Takimini's
fanning himself, the Doll's wound up.
(Imary returns to his apartment.)
Larivaudière, magnetic, and Pitou
lie there, skewed. My Man Friday
dreams of green islands and dances no more.

Lindau

La rondine vi porta
fili d'erba, non vuole che la vita passi.
Ma tra gli argini, a notte, l'acqua morta
logora i sassi.
Sotto le torce fumicose sbanda
sempre qualche ombra sulle prode vuote.
Nel cerchio della piazza una sarabanda
s'agita al mugghio dei battelli a ruote.

Lindau

The swallow bringing in wisps
of grass doesn't want this life to end.
But in between the banks, at night, dead water
saps the stones.
Under smoking torches a few shadows scatter
on the deserted shores. In the circle
of the piazza, a saraband beats time
to the rumble of the paddle wheels.

Bagni di Lucca

Fra il tonfo dei marroni
e il gemito del torrente
che uniscono i loro suoni
èsita il cuore.

Precoce inverno che borea
abbrividisce. M'affaccio
sul ciglio che scioglie l'albore
del giorno nel ghiaccio.

Marmi, rameggi—
                  e ad uno scrollo giù
foglie a èlice, a freccia,
nel fossato.

Passa l'ultima greggia nella nebbia
del suo fiato.

Bagni di Lucca

Between the chestnuts thudding
down and the torrent's wail,
all one sound,
the heart falters.

Early winter shuddering
in the north wind. I lean over
the ledge where the day's first white
light dissolves in ice.

Marblings, branchings—
                              and suddenly, shaken loose,
leaves spiraling, arrowing down
into the ditch.

The last herd passes in the mist
of its own breathing.

Cave d'autunno

su cui discende la primavera lunare
e nimba di candore ogni frastaglio,
schianti di pigne, abbaglio
di reti stese e schegge,

ritornerà ritornerà sul gelo
la bontà d'una mano,
varcherà il cielo lontano
la ciurma luminosa che ci saccheggia.

Autumn Cellars

on which the lunar spring descends,
blanching every shard with halo splendor,
chips of broken cones, sheen
of drying nets, splinters,

back to us, across the cold,
will come the bounty of a hand,
shining over the far horizon will come
the white horde, to loot and plunder.

Altro effetto di luna

La trama del carrubo che si profila
nuda contro l'azzurro sonnolento,
il suono delle voci, la trafila
delle dita d'argento sulle soglie,

la piuma che s'invischia, un trepestìo
sul molo che si scioglie
e la feluca già ripiega il volo
con le vele dimesse come spoglie.

Another Moon Effect

The carob's web in naked
profile against the drowsing blue,
voices calling, silver fingers
slipping over the sills,

the feather snagged, a trampling
on the wharf that slides away,
and the felucca, sails luffing like a dress,
comes about, on her fresh tack.

Verso Vienna

Il convento barocco
di schiuma e di biscotto
adombrava uno scorcio d'acque lente
e tavole imbandite, qua e là sparse
di foglie e zenzero.

Emerse un nuotatore, sgrondò sotto
una nube di moscerini,
chiese del nostro viaggio,
parlò a lungo del suo d'oltre confine.

Additò il ponte in faccia che si passa
(informò) con un soldo di pedaggio.
Salutò con la mano, sprofondò,
fu la corrente stessa . . .
                                    Ed al suo posto,
battistrada balzò da una rimessa
un bassotto festoso che latrava,

fraterna unica voce dentro l'afa.

On the Road to Vienna

The baroque convent,
all biscuit and foam,
shaded a glimpse of slow waters
and tables already set, scattered here and there
with leaves and ginger.

A swimmer emerged, dripping
under a cloud of gnats,
inquired about our journey, spoke
at length about his own, beyond the frontier.

He pointed to the bridge before us,
you cross over (he said) with a penny toll.
With a wave of his hand, he sank down,
became the river itself . . .
                            And in his place,
to announce our coming, out of a shed
bounced a dachshund, gaily barking—

sole brotherly voice in the sticky heat.

Carnevale di Gerti

Se la ruota s'impiglia nel groviglio
delle stelle filanti ed il cavallo
s'impenna tra la calca, se ti nevica
sui capelli e le mani un lungo brivido
d'iridi trascorrenti o alzano i bimbi
le flebili ocarine che salutano
il tuo viaggio ed i lievi echi si sfaldano
giù dal ponte sul fiume,
se si sfolla la strada e ti conduce
in un mondo soffiato entro una tremula
bolla d'aria e di luce dove il sole
saluta la tua grazia—hai ritrovato
forse la strada che tentò un istante
il piombo fuso a mezzanotte quando
finì l'anno tranquillo senza spari.

Ed ora vuoi sostare dove un filtro
fa spogli i suoni
e ne deriva i sorridenti ed acri
fumi che ti compongono il domani:
ora chiedi il paese dove gli onagri
mordano quadri di zucchero alle tue mani
e i tozzi alberi spuntino germogli
miracolosi al becco dei pavoni.

(Oh il tuo Carnevale sarà più triste
stanotte anche del mio, chiusa fra i doni
tu per gli assenti: carri dalle tinte
di rosolio, fantocci ed archibugi,
palle di gomma, arnesi da cucina
lillipuziani: l'urna li segnava
a ognuno dei lontani amici l'ora
che il Gennaio si schiuse e nel silenzio
si compì il sortilegio. È Carnevale
o il Dicembre s'indugia ancora? Penso
che se tu muovi la lancetta al piccolo.

Gerti's Carnival

Should the wheel snag in a swirl
of shooting stars and the horse
rear in the crowd, should a long shudder
of fading iridescence snow your hair
and hands, or the children lift
mourning ocarinas to salute you
as you pass, and gentle echoes
flake from the bridge down to the river below,
should the road, empty of people, lead you out
to a world blown to a shimmering
bubble, all air and light, where the sun
hails your grace—maybe then you'll have found
the road the molten lead had hinted at
for one minute, at midnight, when the tranquil year
ended, without a shot.

And now you'd rather be where a filter
sifts the sounds,
sucking from them the fumes, sweet
and bitter, of which your future's made:
now you seek that land where onagers
nibble lumps of sugar from your hands,
where stunted trees sprout miraculous
buds for the peacock's beak.

(Ah, your Carnival tonight will be even sadder
than mine—you shut in among your gifts
for those who aren't there: rosolio-colored
carts, Raggedy Anns, arquebuses,
rubber balls, and Lilliputian
pots and pans: one assigned
to each of your distant friends the instant
January was revealed, the lots
silently cast. Is it Carnival yet,
or December lingering on? Merely turn
the stem of that little watch

orologio che rechi al polso, tutto
arretrerà dentro un disfatto prisma
babelico di forme e di colori . . .)

E il Natale verrà e il giorno dell'Anno
che sfolla le caserme e ti riporta
gli amici spersi, e questo Carnevale
pur esso tornerà che ora ci sfugge
tra i muri che si fendono già. Chiedi
tu di fermare il tempo sul paese
che attorno si dilata? Le grandi ali
screziate ti sfiorano, le logge
sospingono all'aperto esili bambole
bionde, vive, le pale dei mulini
rotano fisse sulle pozze garrule.
Chiedi di trattenere le campane
d'argento sopra il borgo e il suono rauco
delle colombe? Chiedi tu i mattini
trepidi delle tue prode lontane?

Come tutto si fa strano e difficile,
come tutto è impossibile, tu dici.
La tua vita è quaggiù dove rimbombano
le ruote dei carriaggi senza posa
e nulla torna se non forse in questi
disguidi del possibile. Ritorna
là fra i morti balocchi ove è negato
pur morire; e col tempo che ti batte
al polso e all'esistenza ti ridona,
tra le mura pesanti che non s'aprono
al gorgo degli umani affaticato,
torna alla via dove con te intristisco,
quella che additò un piombo raggelato
alle mie, alle tue sere:
torna alle primavere che non fioriscono.

on your wrist, and everything, I think,
will crumble into a shattered Babel
prism of forms and colors . . .)

And Christmas will come and New Year's Day
that empties the barracks and once again brings back
your scattered friends, and even this Carnival
which now, behind walls beginning to crack, eludes us,
will someday come again. Do you want
time to stop still over the country opening up
around you? The great mottled wings
graze you, loggias thrust
blond, slim, flesh-and-blood dolls
out into the open, the shafts of mill wheels
turning steadily over chattering ponds.
Do you want the silver bells
atop the village to stop, and the throaty cooing
of the doves? Do you seek the shivering
mornings of your distant shores?

How strange, you say, how difficult everything
becomes, how impossible it all is!
Your life is here, down here where the carriage wheels
go rumbling by, never stopping,
where nothing returns except in these
misdirections of the possible. Return, come back
here among these dead toys where even dying's
denied; come back within the time that ticks
on your wrist, that returns you to existence
behind thick walls that won't open
to the weary maelstrom of men,
come back, here where I sadden at your side, to the road
at which the molten lead, hardening, hinted,
to our evenings, yours, mine,
come back to these unblossoming springs.

Verso Capua

. . . rotto il colmo sull'ansa, con un salto,
il Volturno calò, giallo, la sua
piena tra gli scopeti, la disperse
nelle crete. Laggiù si profilava
mobile sulle siepi un postiglione,
e apparì su cavalli,
in una scia di polvere e sonagli.
Si arrestò pochi istanti, l'equipaggio
dava scosse, d'attorno volitavano
farfalle minutissime. Un furtivo
raggio incendiò di colpo il sughereto
scotennato, a fatica ripartiva
la vettura: e tu in fondo che agitavi
lungamente una sciarpa, la bandiera
stellata!, e il fiume ingordo s'insabbiava.

Toward Capua

. . . its crest broken at the bend, plunging,
the Volturno, yellowish, dropped its torrent
across the heath, dispersing
in clay. Down below, above
the hedgerows a coachman in profile moved
as though riding on horseback
in a wake of dust and jingling bells.
An instant, the carriage stopped, shook,
lurched, and tiny butterflies were
fluttering all about. Suddenly a sly shaft
of sunlight kindled, flaming the cork oaks
in the barked grove; the carriage struggled,
then drove away: and you, inside, you were waving,
waving your scarf, the starry
banner! and the glutton river sank in sand.

A Liuba che parte

Non il grillo ma il gatto
del focolare
or ti consiglia, splendido
lare della dispersa tua famiglia.
La casa che tu rechi
con te ravvolta, gabbia o cappelliera?,
sovrasta i ciechi tempi come il flutto
arca leggera—e basta al tuo riscatto.

To Liuba, Leaving

Not the cricket, but the cat
on the hearth, shining
household god of your scattered clan,
is now your oracle.
The house you carry
snugly around you—bird cage, bandbox?—
rides these blind days, light as an ark
on the tide—enough for your salvation.

Bibe a Ponte all'Asse

Bibe, ospite lieve, la bruna tua reginetta di Saba
mesce sorrisi e Rùfina di quattordici gradi.

Si vede in basso rilucere la terra fra gli àceri radi
e un bimbo curva la canna sul gomito della Greve.

Bibe at Ponte all'Asse

Bibe, merry guest, your little brunette queen of Sheba,
mingles smiles with Rùfina wine, fourteen percent.

Below, through the scattered maples, the earth shimmers,
and a kid's fishing pole arches at the bend of the Greve.

Dora Markus

I

Fu dove il ponte di legno
mette a Porto Corsini sul mare alto
e rari uomini, quasi immoti, affondano
o salpano le reti. Con un segno
della mano additavi all'altra sponda
invisibile la tua patria vera.
Poi seguimmo il canale fino alla darsena
della città, lucida di fuliggine,
nella bassura dove s'affondava
una primavera inerte, senza memoria.

E qui dove un'antica vita
si screzia in una dolce
ansietà d'Oriente,
le tue parole iridavano come le scaglie
della triglia moribonda.

La tua irrequietudine mi fa pensare
agli uccelli di passo che urtano ai fari
nelle sere tempestose:
è una tempesta anche la tua dolcezza,
turbina e non appare,
e i suoi riposi sono anche più rari.
Non so come stremata tu resisti
in questo lago
d'indifferenza ch'è il tuo cuore; forse
ti salva un amuleto che tu tieni
vicino alla matita delle labbra,
al piumino, alla lima: un topo bianco,
d'avorio; e così esisti!

Dora Markus

It was where the wooden bridge
runs to Porto Corsini over open water
and a few men, moving slowly, sink their nets
or haul them in. With a wave
of your hand you pointed toward the invisible
shore beyond, your true fatherland.
Then we followed the canal back to the city's
inner harbor, shining with soot,
in the wet flats where a sluggish springtime
was settling down, unremembering.

And here where an ancient life
is mottled with a sweet
Oriental yearning,
your words shimmered like the scales
of a dying mullet.

Your restlessness reminds me
of those migratory birds that thump against the lighthouse
on stormy nights:
even your sweetness is a storm
whose raging's unseen,
whose lulls are even rarer.
I don't know how, *in extremis,* you resist
in that lake of indifference that is your heart; perhaps
some amulet preserves you,
some keepsake beside your lipstick,
powder puff, or file: a white mouse,
of ivory. And so you persist.

Ormai nella tua Carinzia
di mirti fioriti e di stagni,
china sul bordo sorvegli
la carpa che timida abbocca
o segui sui tigli, tra gl'irti
pinnacoli le accensioni
del vespro e nell'acque un avvampo
di tende da scali e pensioni.

La sera che si protende
sull'umida conca non porta
col palpito dei motori
che gemiti d'oche e un interno
di nivee maioliche dice
allo specchio annerito che ti vide
diversa una storia di errori
imperturbati e la incide
dove la spugna non giunge.

La tua leggenda, Dora!
Ma è scritta già in quegli sguardi
di uomini che hanno fedine
altere e deboli in grandi
ritratti d'oro e ritorna
ad ogni accordo che esprime
l'armonica guasta nell'ora
che abbuia, sempre più tardi.

È scritta là. Il sempreverde
alloro per la cucina
resiste, la voce non muta,
Ravenna è lontana, distilla
veleno una fede feroce.
Che vuole da te? Non si cede
voce, leggenda o destino . . .
Ma è tardi, sempre più tardi.

II

Now in your Carinthia
of flowering myrtles and ponds,
leaning over the edge, you look down
at the shy carp gaping,
or under the lime trees follow the evening
star kindling among the jagged
peaks, and the water aflame with awnings
on lodging houses and piers.

The night that reaches out
over the damp inlet brings,
mingled with throbbing motors,
only the honking of geese; and an interior
of snow-white tiles tells
the blackened mirror that sees the change
in you a tale of errors calmly
accepted, etching it in
where the sponge won't reach.

Your legend, Dora!
But it's written already in the stares
of men with scraggly whiskers, dignified,
in great gilded portraits, returning
in every chord sounded
by the broken street-organ in the darkening
hour, always later.

It's written there. The evergreen
bays for the kitchen
resist, the voice doesn't change.
Ravenna's far away, a brutal
faith distills its venom. What
does it want from you? Voice,
legend, or fate can't be surrendered . . .
But it's getting late, always later.

Alla maniera di Filippo De Pisis
nell'inviargli questo libro

> . . . *l'Arno balsamo fino*
> LAPO GIANNI

Una botta di stocco nel zig zag
del beccaccino—
e si librano piume su uno scrìmolo.

(Poi discendono là, fra sgorbiature
di rami, al freddo balsamo del fiume.)

In the Manner of Filippo De Pisis,
On Sending Him This Book

> *. . . l'Arno balsamo fino*
> LAPO GIANNI

A rapier thrust in the zigzag
of the snipe—
and feathers teeter on a rim.

(Then drift down, among blotches
of boughs, there, in the cold solace of the stream.)

Nel Parco di Caserta

Dove il cigno crudele
si liscia e si contorce,
sul pelo dello stagno, tra il fogliame,
si risveglia una sfera, dieci sfere,
una torcia dal fondo, dieci torce,

—e un sole si bilancia
a stento nella prim'aria,
su domi verdicupi e globi a sghembo
d'araucaria,

che scioglie come liane
braccia di pietra, allaccia
senza tregua chi passa
e ne sfila dal punto più remoto
radici e stame.

Le nòcche delle Madri s'inaspriscono,
cercano il vuoto.

In the Park at Caserta

Where the cruel swan,
contorting, preens himself
on the pond's slick, among the leaves,
a sphere revives, ten spheres,
a torch from the depths, ten torches,

—and a sun teeters,
struggling in the early air, over
green domes and twisted globes
of the monkey-puzzle tree,

which looses stone arms
like creepers, clutching
persistently at every passerby,
from the farthest point unraveling
stamens and roots.

The knuckles of the Mothers roughen,
grope for the void.

Accelerato

Fu così, com'è il brivido
pungente che trascorre
i sobborghi e solleva
alle aste delle torri
la cenere del giorno,
com'è il soffio
piovorno che ripete
tra le sbarre l'assalto
ai salici reclini—
fu così e fu tumulto nella dura
oscurità che rompe
qualche foro d'azzurro finchè lenta
appaia la ninfale
Entella che sommessa
rifluisce dai cieli dell'infanzia
oltre il futuro—
poi vennero altri liti, mutò il vento,
crebbe il bucato ai fili, uomini ancora
uscirono all'aperto, nuovi nidi
turbarono le gronde—
fu così,
rispondi?

Local Train

That's how it was, like the piercing
shudder that slips through
the suburbs, that hoists
the dawn's ashes to the flagstaffs
of the towers,
like the wet wind
gusting through the gratings,
assaulting
the bent willows—
that's how it was, turmoil in the bitter
darkness broken by
a few slits of blue until the apparition slowly
rose, the nymph Entella, flowing softly
from childhood horizons lying
beyond the future—
then other coasts slid by, the wind changed,
more laundry on the lines, men ventured out
once more, new nests
agitated the gutters—
and that's how it was,
you answer?

II

Motets

Sobre el volcán la flor.
G. A. BÉCQUER

Lo sai: debbo riperderti e non posso

Lo sai: debbo riperderti e non posso.
Come un tiro aggiustato mi sommuove
ogni opera, ogni grido e anche lo spiro
salino che straripa
dai moli e fa l'oscura primavera
di Sottoripa.

Paese di ferrame e alberature
a selva nella polvere del vespro.
Un ronzìo lungo viene dall'aperto,
strazia com'unghia ai vetri. Cerco il segno
smarrito, il pegno solo ch'ebbi in grazia
da te.
      E l'inferno è certo.

You know: I must leave you again . . .

You know: I must leave you again and I can't.
Like a well-targeted shot, every effort,
every cry, unsettles me, even the salt
breeze overflowing
from the quays that makes Sottoripa's
springtime so dark.

Land of iron and masts
forested in the evening dust.
A long droning comes from open space,
screeches like a fingernail on glass. I look for the lost
sign, the only pledge I had of your
grace.
      And hell is certain.

Molti anni, e uno più duro sopra il lago

Molti anni, e uno più duro sopra il lago
straniero su cui ardono i tramonti.
Poi scendesti dai monti a riportarmi
San Giorgio e il Drago.

Imprimerli potessi sul palvese
che s'agita alla frusta del grecale
in cuore . . . E per te scendere in un gorgo
di fedeltà, immortale.

Many years, and one year harder still . . .

Many years, and one year harder still on the foreign
lake aflame with the setting sun. Then
you came down from the hills, you brought me back
my native Saint George and the Dragon.

If only I could print them on this blazon
thrashing under the lash of the northeaster
in my heart . . . And then, for your sake, sink
in a whirlpool of fidelity, undying.

Brina sui vetri; uniti

Brina sui vetri; uniti
sempre e sempre in disparte
gl'infermi; e sopra i tavoli
i lunghi soliloqui sulle carte.

Fu il tuo esilio. Ripenso
anche al mio, alla mattina
quando udii tra gli scogli crepitare
la bomba ballerina.

E durarono a lungo i notturni giuochi
di Bengala: come in una festa.

È scorsa un'ala rude, t'ha sfiorato le mani,
ma invano: la tua carta non è questa.

Frost on the panes . . .

Frost on the panes, the sick
always together and always kept
apart; and over the tables long
soliloquies about cards.

That was your exile. I think again
of mine, of the morning
among the cliffs when I heard the crackle
of the ballerina bomb.

And the fireworks went on
and on: as though it were a holiday.

A brutal wing slid past, it grazed your hands,
but nothing more. That card isn't yours.

Lontano, ero con te quando tuo padre

Lontano, ero con te quando tuo padre
entrò nell'ombra e ti lasciò il suo addio.
Che seppi fino allora? Il logorìo
di *prima* mi salvò solo per questo:

che t'ignoravo e non dovevo: ai colpi
d'oggi lo so, se di laggiù s'inflette
un'ora e mi riporta Cumerlotti
o Anghébeni—tra scoppi di spolette
e i lamenti e l'accorrer delle squadre.

Though far away, I was with you . . .

Though far away, I was with you when your father
passed into shadow and left you his farewell.
What did I know till then? The wear and tear
of *before* preserved me only for this:

that I didn't know you, and that I should have. This
I know from today's barrage, when one hour of hell
forces me back in time, brings back Cumerlotti
or Anghébeni again—the mines exploding,
the moaning, and the bomb squads scrambling up.

Addii, fischi nel buio, cenni, tosse

Addii, fischi nel buio, cenni, tosse
e sportelli abbassati. È l'ora. Forse
gli automi hanno ragione. Come appaiono
dai corridoi, murati!

—Presti anche tu alla fioca
litania del tuo rapido quest'orrida
e fedele cadenza di carioca?—

Goodbyes, whistles in the dark . . .

Goodbyes, whistles in the dark, hands waving, coughing,
train windows lowered. All aboard! Maybe
the robots are right. From the corridors
how incarcerated they seem!

—Is there even something of you in your train's
hoarse litany, this horrible,
faithful carioca beat?—

La speranza di pure rivederti

La speranza di pure rivederti
m'abbandonava;

e mi chiesi se questo che mi chiude
ogni senso di te, schermo d'immagini,
ha i segni della morte o dal passato
è in esso, ma distorto e fatto labile,
un *tuo* barbaglio:

(a Modena, tra i portici,
un servo gallonato trascinava
due sciacalli al guinzaglio.)

The hope of even seeing you . . .

The hope of even seeing you again
was slipping from me;

and I asked myself if what sunders me
from any sense of you, this scrim of images,
bears the signs of death, or if, out of the past,
it still preserves, elusive, blurred,
some brightness of *you*:

(At Modena, among the porticoes,
a flunky in gold braid was tugging
two jackals on a leash.)

Il saliscendi bianco e nero dei

Il saliscendi bianco e nero dei
balestrucci dal palo
del telegrafo al mare
non conforta i tuoi crucci su lo scalo
né ti riporta dove più non sei.

Già profuma il sambuco fitto su
lo sterrato; il piovasco si dilegua.
Se il chiarore è una tregua,
la tua cara minaccia la consuma.

The soaring-dipping white and black . . .

The soaring-dipping white and black
of the martins flying from the telegraph
pole seaward
doesn't soothe your distress on the pier
or bring you back where you no longer are.

Already the elder's heavy perfume hovers
over the dirt road; the shower relents.
If this brightness is a truce,
your beloved menace consumes it.

Ecco il segno; s'innerva

Ecco il segno; s'innerva
sul muro che s'indora:
un frastaglio di palma
bruciato dai barbagli dell'aurora.

Il passo che proviene
dalla serra sì lieve,
non è felpato dalla neve, è ancora
tua vita, sangue tuo nelle mie vene.

Here's the sign . . .

Here's the sign brightening
on the wall, the wall gone golden:
jagged edges of the palm
scorched by the sun's blazing.

The step moving
so lightly from the greenhouse
isn't muffled by snow, it's still
your life, your blood in my veins.

Il ramarro, se scocca

Il ramarro, se scocca
sotto la grande fersa
dalle stoppie—

la vela, quando fiotta
e s'inabissa al salto
della rocca—

il cannone di mezzodì
più fioco del tuo cuore
e il cronometro se
scatta senza rumore—

★ ★ ★

e poi? Luce di lampo
invano può mutarvi in alcunché
di ricco e strano. Altro era il tuo stampo.

The green lizard if it darts . . .

The green lizard if it darts
under the great flail
from the stubble—

the sail, when it flaps
and founders on the up-
towering rock—

the noon cannon
fainter than your heart,
and the clock, if it strikes
without a sound—

★ ★ ★

what then? In vain can the lightning
change you into something rich
and strange. You were stamped from another mold.

Perché tardi? Nel pino lo scoiattolo

Perché tardi? Nel pino lo scoiattolo
batte la coda a torcia sulla scorza.
La mezzaluna scende col suo picco
nel sole che la smorza. È giorno fatto.

A un soffio il pigro fumo trasalisce,
si difende nel punto che ti chiude.
Nulla finisce, o tutto, se tu fólgore
lasci la nube.

Why do you delay? . . .

Why do you delay? The squirrel in the pine
flicks his torch-tail against the bark.
The half-moon with her horns sinks, paling
into the sun. The day is done.

At a puff the sluggish smoke leaps up,
sheltering the point enclosing you.
Nothing—or everything—is over,
O lightning, if you leave your cloud.

L'anima che dispensa

L'anima che dispensa
furlana e rigodone ad ogni nuova
stagione della stranda, s'alimenta
della chiusa passione, la ritrova
a ogni angolo più intensa.

La tua voce è quest'anima diffusa.
Su fili, su ali, al vento, a caso, col
favore della musa o d'un ordegno,
ritorna lieta o triste. Parlo d'altro,
ad altri che t'ignora e il suo disegno
è là che insiste *do re la sol sol* . . .

The soul dispensing reels . . .

The soul dispensing
reels and rigadoons at each fresh
season of the journey feeds on
secret passion, finds it again
at every turn, more intense.

Your voice is this soul diffusing.
On wires, on wings, in the wind, by chance,
by the Muses' grace or some contrivance,
sad or gay, it keeps returning. I speak of other things
to those who don't know you, and its design
is there, insisting: *do re la sol sol* . . .

Ti libero la fronte dai ghiaccioli

Ti libero la fronte dai ghiaccioli
che raccogliesti traversando l'alte
nebulose; hai le penne lacerate
dai cicloni, ti desti a soprassalti.

Mezzodì: allunga nel riquadro il nespolo
l'ombra nera, s'ostina in cielo un sole
freddoloso; e l'altre ombre che scantonano
nel vicolo non sanno che sei qui.

I free your forehead . . .

I free your forehead from the icicles
you gathered crossing the milky
heights; your wings were shattered
by cyclones; you wake with a start.

Noon: the black shadow of the medlar
lengthens in the court; overhead a chilling sun
persists; and the other shades rounding the corner
of the alley don't know you're here.

La gondola che scivola in un forte

La gondola che scivola in un forte
bagliore di catrame e di papaveri,
la subdola canzone che s'alzava
da masse di cordame, l'alte porte
rinchiuse su di te e risa di maschere
che fuggivano a frotte—

una sera tra mille e la mia notte
è più profonda! S'agita laggiù
uno smorto groviglio che m'avviva
a stratti e mi fa eguale a quell'assorto
pescatore d'anguille dalla riva.

The gondola gliding . . .

The gondola gliding in a bright
blaze of tar oil and poppies, the sly song
that rose from piles of coiled
rope, the great high doors shut
against you, laughter of maskers
running off in hordes—

one evening out of thousands, and my night
is deeper still. Below, there stirs
a blurred tangle that startles me awake,
making me one with the man on the bank
intently angling for eels.

Infuria sale o grandine? Fa strage

Infuria sale o grandine? Fa strage
di campanule, svelle la cedrina.
Un rintocco subacqueo s'avvicina,
quale tu lo destavi, e s'allontana.

La pianola degl'inferi da sé
accelera i registri, sale nelle
sfere del gelo . . . —brilla come te
quando fingevi col tuo trillo d'aria
Lakmé nell'Aria delle Campanelle.

Is it salt or hail that rages? . . .

Is it salt or hail that rages? It batters
the bellflowers down, tears up the verbena.
An underwater knell, aroused by you,
draws closer, then dies in the distance.

On its own, the pianola of the underworld
quickens, changes pitch, soars into
spheres of ice . . . glitters like you,
when, all airy trilling, you sang
Lakmé in the "Bell Song."

Al primo chiaro, quando

Al primo chiaro, quando
subitaneo un rumore
di ferrovia mi parla
di chiusi uomini in corsa
nel traforo del sasso
illuminato a tagli
da cieli ed acque misti;

al primo buio, quando
il bulino che tarla
la scrivanìa rafforza
il suo fervore e il passo
del guardiano s'accosta:
al chiaro e al buio, soste ancora umane
se tu a intrecciarle col tuo refe insisti.

At first light . . .

At first light, when
suddenly the sound
of a train speak to me
of men shut in, in transit
through stone tunnels
lighted by slits
of sky and water meeting;

at first dark, when
the burin gnawing
at the desk doubles
its zeal and the guard's
steps draw closer:
at dawn, at dusk, pauses still human
if you persist, weaving in your thread.

Il fiore che ripete

Il fiore che ripete
dall'orlo del burrato
non scordarti di me,
non ha tinte più liete né più chiare
dello spazio gettato tra me e te.

Un cigolìo si sferra, ci discosta,
l'azzurro pervicace non ricompare.
Nell'afa quasi visibile mi riporta all'opposta
tappa, già buia, la funicolare.

The flower on the cliff's edge . . .

The flower on the cliff's
edge with its refrain
forget-me-not
has no colors brighter, more gay,
than the space flung down between you and me.

A sound of cranking, we're wrenched apart,
the stubborn-seeming sky begins to fade.
In almost visible heat, the cable car lowers me
down to the bottom, where it's dark.

La rana, prima a ritentar la corda

La rana, prima a ritentar la corda
dallo stagno che affossa
giunchi e nubi, stormire dei carrubi
conserti dove spenge le sue fiaccole
un sole senza caldo, tardo ai fiori
ronzìo di coleotteri che suggono
ancora linfe, ultimi suoni, avara
vita della campagna. Con un soffio
l'ora s'estingue: un cielo di lavagna
si prepara a un irrompere di scarni
cavalli, alle scintille degli zoccoli.

First the frog . . .

First the frog, testing a chord
out of the marsh where haze and bulrushes
ditch together, rustle of plaited
carobs where a sun almost cold quenches
its last flickering light, late droning
of coleopters at the flowers, still
sucking sap, last sounds, the country's greedy
life. A puff, and the hour's
out: a slate sky
braces against the charge of famished
horses, the sparking of their hooves.

Non recidere, forbice, quel volto

Non recidere, forbice, quel volto,
solo nella memoria che si sfolla,
non far del grande suo viso in ascolto
la mia nebbia di sempre.

Un freddo cala . . . Duro il colpo svetta.
E l'acacia ferita da sé scrolla
il guscio di cicala
nella prima belletta di Novembre.

Scissors, don't cut that face . . .

Scissors, don't cut that face,
all that's left in my thinning memory.
Don't change her great listening look
into my everlasting blur.

A chill strikes . . . The harsh blow slices.
And the acacia, wounded, peels off
the cicada's husk
in the first November mud.

La canna che dispiuma

La canna che dispiuma
mollemente il suo rosso
flabello a primavera;
la rèdola nel fosso, su la nera
correntìa sorvolata di libellule;
e il cane trafelato che rincasa
col suo fardello in bocca,

oggi qui non mi tocca riconoscere;
ma là dove il riverbero più cuoce
e il nuvolo s'abbassa, oltre le sue
pupille ormai remote, solo due
fasci di luce in croce.
                    E il tempo passa.

The reed that softly sheds . . .

The reed that softly
sheds its red feather-fan
in spring;
the grassy path along the ditch above the black
stream where dragonflies hover
and the dog that comes panting home,
its bundle in its teeth,

here, today, I needn't recognize;
but there where the glare burns hottest
and the cloud descends, beyond
her eyes now far away, nothing but two
beams of light, crossing.
                    And time goes on.

. . . ma così sia. Un suono di cornetta

. . . ma così sia. Un suono di cornetta
dialoga con gli sciami del querceto.
Nella valva che il vespero riflette
un vulcano dipinto fuma lieto.

La moneta incassata nella lava
brilla anch'essa sul tavolo e trattiene
pochi fogli. La vita che sembrava
vasta è più breve del tuo fazzoletto.

. . . but let it be. . . .

. . . but let it be. A blowing bugle
converses with the swarms among the oaks.
In the shell where the evening star is mirrored
a painted volcano happily smokes.

The coin imbedded in lava
also shines on the tabletop, weighting a few scraps
of paper. Life, which once seemed so vast,
is smaller than your handkerchief.

III

Tempi di Bellosguardo

Oh come là nella corusca
distesa che s'inarca verso i colli,
il brusìo della sera s'assottiglia
e gli alberi discorrono col trito
mormorio della rena; come limpida
s'inalvea là in decoro
di colonne e di salci ai lati e grandi salti
di lupi nei giardini, tra le vasche ricolme
che traboccano,
questa vita di tutti non più posseduta
del nostro respiro;
e come si ricrea una luce di zàffiro
per gli uomini
che vivono laggiù: è troppo triste
che tanta pace illumini a spiragli
e tutto ruoti poi con rari guizzi
su l'anse vaporanti, con incroci
di camini, con grida dai giardini
pensili, con sgomenti e lunghe risa
sui tetti ritagliati, tra le quinte
dei frondami ammassati ed una coda
fulgida che trascorra in cielo prima
che il desiderio trovi le parole!

Bellosguardo Times

Ah, down there in the shining
expanse that arches toward the hills,
how the hum of evening thins away
and the trees converse with the weary chatter
of the sandbanks; how limpidly
the life of everything, no longer possessed
by our breathing, carves its channel through
stateliness of columns, aisles of willows, the wolves'
giant leaping in the gardens, brimming urns
spilling over; and
how a sapphire light shines afresh
for all men living
down there. Sad, so sad
that a peace like this should lighten only by glints
and everything, with a few shimmerings, turn back
across the misting loops, intersected
by chimneys, and cries from terraced
gardens, by alarms and loud laughter
from hard-edged roofs, between wings
of massing branches and a tail of light
that crosses over to heaven before
desire finds words!

Derelitte sul poggio
fronde della magnolia
verdibrune se il vento
porta dai frigidari
dei pianterreni un travolto
concitamento d'accordi
ed ogni foglia che oscilla
o rilampeggia nel folto
in ogni fibra s'imbeve
di quel saluto, e più ancora
derelitte le fronde
dei vivi che si smarriscono
nel prisma del minuto,
le membra di febbre votate
al moto che si ripete
in circolo breve: sudore
che pulsa, sudore di morte,
atti minuti specchiati,
sempre gli stessi, rifranti
echi del batter che in alto
sfaccetta il sole e la pioggia,
fugace altalena tra vita
che passa e vita che sta,
quassù non c'è scampo: si muore
sapendo o si sceglie la vita
che muta ed ignora: altra morte.
E scende la cuna tra logge
ed erme: l'accordo commuove
le lapidi che hanno veduto
le immagini grandi, l'onore,
l'amore inflessibile, il giuoco,
la fedeltà che non muta.
E il gesto rimane: misura
il vuoto, ne sonda il confine:
il gesto ignoto che esprime
se stesso e non altro: passione
di sempre in un sangue e un cervello
irripetuti; e fors'entra
nel chiuso e lo forza con l'esile
sua punta di grimaldello.

★ ★ ★

Derelict on the slope
green-brown magnolia leaves
when the wind from icy
ground-floor rooms
carries up a jumbled
concitation of chords
and every leaf shaking
or shining in the dense thicket
drinks that greeting in
at every fiber; and still more
derelict the leaves
of the living, lost
in the prism of the instant,
limbs of fever dedicated
to that movement which, in brief
cycle, repeats itself: sweat
throbbing, death sweat,
acts moments mirrored,
always the same, echoes refracted
from the buffeting above that makes
facets of sun and rain, swing
that sways between life
passing and life persisting,
up here there's no escape: we die
and know it or we choose the life that changes
and doesn't know: a different death.
And the cradle falls among balconies
and herms: the harmony stirs
stones that have seen
the great images, honor,
unbending love, the rules of the game,
fidelity unaltering.
And the gesture holds: it measures out
the void, sounds its boundaries:
the unknown gesture expressive
of itself and nothing else: passion
of forever in a blood and brain
never to be repeated; and maybe it works its way
into the closure with fine picklock point
and pries it open.

Il rumore degli émbrici distrutti
dalla bufera
nell'aria dilatata che non s'incrina,
l'inclinarsi del pioppo
del Canadà, tricuspide, che vibra
nel giardino a ogni strappo—
e il segno di una vita che assecondi
il marmo a ogni scalino come l'edera
diffida dello slancio solitario
dei ponti che discopro da quest'altura;
d'una clessidra che non sabbia ma opere
misuri e volti umani, piante umane;
d'acque composte sotto padiglioni
e non più irose a ritentar fondali
di pomice, è sparito? Un suono lungo
dànno le terrecotte, i pali appena
difendono le ellissi dei convolvoli,
e le locuste arrancano piovute
sui libri dalle pergole; dura opera,
tessitrici celesti, ch'è interrotta
sul telaio degli uomini. E domani . . .

★ ★ ★

Sound of roof tiles being ripped apart
by the gusting storm
that taut air that widens out, uncracking,
the slanting of the garden's
Canada poplar, three-pointed, shaking
at every wrench—
and the sign of a life that accommodates
the marble at every step like the ivy
flinching from the solitary thrust of the bridges
I descry from this high outlook here:
sign of an hourglass that measures not sand
but human works and faces, human plants;
sign of waters under summerhouses, composed,
no longer raging to plumb the depths
of pumice, has the sign vanished? The terracotta tiles
give a long screech, the stakes barely hold
the bindweed's clutching tendrils
and the locusts that pelted down
on the books in the arbor hobble about: hard work,
heavenly weavers, interrupted
on the looms of men. And tomorrow . . .

IV

Sap check'd with frost, and lusty leaves quite gone,
Beauty o'ersnow'd and bareness every where.

SHAKESPEARE, Sonnets, V

La casa dei doganieri

Tu non ricordi la casa dei doganieri
sul rialzo a strapiombo sulla scogliera:
desolata t'attende dalla sera
in cui v'entrò lo sciame dei tuoi pensieri
e vi sostò irrequieto.

Libeccio sferza da anni le vecchie mura
e il suono del tuo riso non è più lieto:
la bussola va impazzita all'avventura
e il calcolo dei dadi più non torna.
Tu non ricordi; altro tempo frastorna
la tua memoria; un filo s'addipana.

Ne tengo ancora un capo; ma s'allontana
la casa e in cima al tetto la banderuola
affumicata gira senza pietà.
Ne tengo un capo; ma tu resti sola
né qui respiri nell'oscurità.

Oh l'orizzonte in fuga, dove s'accende
rara la luce della petroliera!
Il varco è qui? (Ripullula il frangente
ancora sulla balza che scoscende . . .)
Tu non ricordi la casa di questa
mia sera. Ed io non so chi va e chi resta.

The Coastguard Station

You don't remember the coastguard house
perched at the top of the jutting height,
awaiting you still, abandoned since that night
when your thoughts came swarming in
and paused there, hovering.

Southwesters have lashed the old walls for years,
the gaiety has vanished from your laugh:
the compass swings at random, crazy,
odds can no longer be laid on the dice.
You don't remember: other days trouble
your memory: a thread pays out.

I hold one end still; but the house
keeps receding, above the roof the soot-
blackened weathervane whirls, pitiless.
I hold one end: but you stay on, alone, not
here, breathing in my darkness.

Oh, the horizon keeps on receding, there, far out
where a rare tanker's light blinks in the blackness!
Is the crossing here? (The furious breakers
climb the cliff that falls off, sheer . . .)
You don't remember the house of this, my evening.
And I don't know who's staying, who's leaving.

Bassa marea

Sere di gridi, quando l'altalena
oscilla nella pergola d'allora
e un oscuro vapore vela appena
la fissità del mare.

Non più quel tempo. Varcano ora il muro
rapidi voli obliqui, la discesa
di tutto non s'arresta e si confonde
sulla proda scoscesa anche lo scoglio
che ti portò primo sull'onde.

Viene col soffio della primavera
un lugubre risucchio
d'assorbite esistenze; e nella sera,
negro vilucchio, solo il tuo ricordo
s'attorce e si difende.

S'alza sulle spallette, sul tunnel più lunge
dove il treno lentissimo s'imbuca.
Una mandria lunare sopraggiunge
poi sui colli, invisibile, e li bruca.

Low Tide

Evenings of cries, when the swing
rocks in the summerhouse of other days
and a dark vapor barely veils
the sea's fixity.

Those days are gone. Now swift flights
slant across the wall, the plummeting
of everything goes on and on, the steep coast
swallows even the reef that first lifted you
above the waves.

With the breath of spring comes
a mournful undertow of lives
engulfed; and in the evening,
black bindweed, only your memory
writhes and resists.

Rises over the embankments, the distant tunnel
where the train, slowly crawling, enters.
Then, unseen, a lunar flock comes drifting in
to browse on the hills.

Stanze

Ricerco invano il punto onde si mosse
il sangue che ti nutre, interminato
respingersi di cerchi oltre lo spazio
breve dei giorni umani,
che ti rese presente in uno strazio
d'agonie che non sai, viva in un putre
padule d'astro inabissato; ed ora
è linfa che disegna le tue mani,
ti batte ai polsi inavvertita e il volto
t'infiamma o discolora.

Pur la rete minuta dei tuoi nervi
rammenta un poco questo suo viaggio
e se gli occhi ti scopro li consuma
un fervore coperto da un passaggio
turbinoso di spuma ch'or s'infitta
ora si frange, e tu lo senti ai rombi
delle tempie vanir nella tua vita
come si rompe a volte nel silenzio
d'una piazza assopita
un volo strepitoso di colombi.

In te converge, ignara, una raggèra
di fili; e certo alcuno d'essi apparve
ad altri: e fu chi abbrividì la sera
percosso da una candida ala in fuga,
e fu chi vide vagabonde larve
dove altri scorse fanciullette a sciami,
o scoperse, qual lampo che dirami,
nel sereno una ruga e l'urto delle
leve del mondo apparse da uno strappo
dell'azzurro l'avvolse, lamentoso.

In te m'appare un'ultima corolla
di cenere leggera che non dura
ma sfioccata precipita. Voluta,

Stanzas

I seek in vain that point from which
the blood you're nourished by began, circles pushing
each other on into infinite space, on
beyond the tiny span
of human days, that made of you a presence
in a rending agony you never knew, living
in this rotting swamp of foundered star. And now
lymph, not blood, invisibly
traces your hands, pounds at your pulses,
flames or blanches your face.

And yet, that subtle network of your nerves
remembers something of its journey,
and if I open your eyes, a blaze
concealed by a surge of angry foam,
curdling, then breaking, consumes them,
and you sense its passage in the pulsing
of your temples, feel it vanishing into your life,
as when the silence of a drowsing
piazza is sometimes shattered
by an explosion of doves.

In you, unaware, an aureole
of rays converges; and surely some of these were seen
by others. And there was one who shuddered
at night, clipped by a white wing brushing by,
and another who saw ghosts wandering
where others saw swarms of young girls,
or discerned, like lightning branching,
the clear sky wrinkle, and the shock
of the world's gears, glimpsed through a crack
in the blue, pulled him in, grieving.

In you I seem to see a last
corolla of fine ash crumble into falling
flakes. Willed,

disvoluta è così la tua natura.
Tocchi il segno, travàlichi. Oh il ronzìo
dell'arco ch'è scoccato, il solco che ara
il flutto e si rinchiude! Ed ora sale
l'ultima bolla in su. La dannazione
è forse questa vaneggiante amara
oscurità che scende su chi resta.

unwilled, this is your nature. You hit
the mark, you overshoot it. Ah, that twang
of the taut bow shot, furrow that plows
the waves, then closes over! And now
the last bubble rises. Maybe damnation
is this wild, bitter blindness descending
on the one who's left behind.

Sotto la pioggia

Un murmure; e la tua casa s'appanna
come nella bruma del ricordo—
e lacrima la palma ora che sordo
preme il disfacimento che ritiene
nell'afa delle serre anche le nude
speranze ed il pensiero che rimorde.

"Por amor de la fiebre" . . . mi conduce
un vortice con te. Raggia vermiglia
una tenda, una finestra si rinchiude.
Sulla rampa materna ora cammina,
guscio d'uovo che va tra la fanghiglia,
poca vita tra sbatter d'ombra e luce.

Strideva Adiós muchachos, compañeros
de mi vida, il tuo disco dalla corte:
e m'è cara la maschera se ancora
di là dal mulinello della sorte
mi rimane il sobbalzo che riporta
al tuo sentiero.

Seguo i lucidi strosci e in fondo, a nembi,
il fumo strascicato d'una nave.
Si punteggia uno squarcio . . .
                              Per te intendo
ciò che osa la cicogna quando alzato
il volo dalla cuspide nebbiosa
rèmiga verso la Città del Capo.

In the Rain

A murmur: and your apartment blurs
and fades as in the haze of memory—
and tears drip from the palms while the grim
obliteration presses down, sealing hope
stripped bare and the torturing thought
in sultry greenhouse heat.

"Por amor de la fiebre" . . . I'm whirled
about at your side. A curtain flares
vermilion, a window slides shut.
Now, along the maternal slope, a white
eggshell on the ooze, in flickering
light and shadow, goes a hint of life.

Your record screeched in the courtyard,
Adiós muchachos, compañeros de mi vida:
and I accept my role provided,
once beyond the whirlpool of my fate,
I'm free to make the leap that brings me
back to your path once more.

I track the shining storms and, far below,
in cloud, a ship and its trail of vapor.
A patchy rift appears . . .
                    Through you I know
the courage of the stork as he lifts wing,
soaring from a pinnacle in cloud,
and strokes for Capetown.

Punta del Mesco

Nel cielo della cava rigato
all'alba dal volo dritto delle pernici
il fumo delle mine s'intenerIva,
saliva lento le pendici a piombo.
Dal rostro del palabotto si capovolsero
le ondine trombettiere silenziose
e affondarono rapide tra le spume
che il tuo passo sfiorava.

Vedo il sentiero che percorsi un giorno
come un cane inquieto; lambe il fiotto,
s'inerpica tra i massi e rado strame
a tratti lo scancella. E tutto è uguale.
Nella ghiaia bagnata s'arrovella
un'eco degli scrosci. Umido brilla
il sole sulle membra affaticate
dei curvi spaccapietre che martellano.

Polene che risalgono e mi portano
qualche cosa di te. Un tràpano incide
il cuore sulla roccia—schianta attorno
più forte un rombo. Brancolo nel fumo,
ma rivedo: ritornano i tuoi rari
gesti e il viso che aggiorna al davanzale,—
mi torna la tua infanzia dilaniata
dagli spari!

Cape Mesco

In the sky over the quarry streaked
at dawn by the partridges' undeviating flight,
the smoke from the blasting thinned,
climbing slowly up the sheer stone face.
From the platform of the piledriver
naiad ripples somersaulted, silent
trumpeters, and sank, melting in the foam
grazed by your step.

I see the path I took one day
like a worried dog; it follows the coast,
clambers among boulders, sometimes disappears
in the stubble. And nothing is changed.
In the damp gravel roils
an echo of thunder. The sodden
sun shines down on the stonecutters' weary bodies
hunching over their hammers.

Figureheads rising, they bring me
something of you. A drill incises
the heart on the stone—a louder blast
crashes all around. I grope in smoke
but once again I see: rare gestures of yours
return, and the face dawning at the window—
and your childhood comes back, tortured
by explosions.

Costa San Giorgio

Un fuoco fatuo impolvera la strada.
Il gasista si cala giù e pedala
rapido con la scala su la spalla.
Risponde un'altra luce e l'ombra attorno
sfarfalla, poi ricade.

Lo so, non s'apre il cerchio
e tutto scende o rapido s'inerpica
tra gli archi. I lunghi mesi
son fuggiti così: ci resta un gelo
fosforico d'insetto nei cunicoli
e un velo scialbo sulla luna.
                        Un dì
brillava sui cammini del prodigio
El Dorado, e fu lutto fra i tuoi padri.
Ora l'Idolo è qui, sbarrato. Tende
le sue braccia fra i càrpini: l'oscuro
ne scancella lo sguardo. Senza voce,
disfatto dall'arsura, quasi esanime,
l'Idolo è in croce.

La sua presenza si diffonde grave.
Nulla ritorna, tutto non veduto
si riforma nel magico falò.
Non c'è respiro; nulla vale: più
non distacca per noi dall'architrave
della stalla il suo lume, Maritornes.

Tutto è uguale; non ridere: lo so,
lo stridere degli anni fin dal primo,
lamentoso, sui cardini, il mattino
un limbo sulla stupida discesa—
e in fondo il torchio del nemico muto
che preme . . .
                        Se una pendola rintocca
dal chiuso porta il tonfo del fantoccio
ch'è abbattuto.

Costa San Giorgio

A will-o'-the-wisp powders the road with dust.
The lamplighter coasts downhill, then pedals
hard, ladder on his shoulder.
A second light responds, the surrounding shadow
flickers, then falls again.

I know, the circle can't be broken,
and between the arcs everything sinks
or suddenly flares up. That's how the long
months raced by, leaving a phosphorescent
ice of insects in the shafts of the mine,
a pale gauze over the moon.
                                    Once
it shone on the path of the prodigious
El Dorado, and there was mourning among your forebears.
Now the Idol's here, barred from us. He reaches out
his arms among the hornbeams: darkness
annuls his gaze. Dumb,
decomposed by heat, lifeless almost,
the Idol's on the cross.

His grave presence is everywhere.
Nothing returns, each unseen thing
is transformed in the magic fire.
No relief; nothing avails: for us
Maritornes no longer unhooks her lantern
from the stable's architrave.

It's all the same; don't laugh: I know it,
from the outset the screak of the years
whining on their hinges, the morning
a limbo on the stupid downward slope—
and at the bottom the screw press of the silent
enemy, turning . . .
                                    If a pendulum strikes
from within, it brings the thud of a puppet
felled.

L'estate

L'ombra crociata del gheppio pare ignota
ai giovinetti arbusti quando rade fugace.
E la nube che vede? Ha tante facce
la polla schiusa.

Forse nel guizzo argenteo della trota
controcorrente
torni anche tu al mio piede fanciulla morta
Aretusa.

Ecco l'òmero acceso, la pepita
travolta al sole,
la cavolaia folle, il filo teso
del ragno su la spuma che ribolle—

e qualcosa che va e tropp'altro che
non passerà la cruna . . .

Occorrono troppe vite per farne una.

Summer

The kestrel's cruciform seems unfamiliar
to the greening bushes grazed by its passing.
And the watching cloud? The welling spring
has so many faces.

Maybe in the silver flash of the trout
swimming upstream, you too
return to my foot, dead maiden
Arethusa.

There's the burnt shoulder, the nugget
upturned to the sun,
the cabbage moth frantic, the spider's thread
taut over the boiling spume—

and something else going by and so much
that won't pass the eye of the needle . . .

Too many lives are needed to make just one.

Eastbourne

"Dio salvi il Re" intonano le trombe
da un padiglione erto su palafitte
che aprono il varco al mare quando sale
a distruggere peste
umide di cavalli nella sabbia
del litorale.

Freddo un vento m'investe
ma un guizzo accende i vetri
e il candore di mica delle rupi
ne risplende.

Bank Holiday . . . Riporta l'onda lunga
della mia vita
a striscio, troppo dolce sulla china.
Si fa tardi. I fragori si distendono,
si chiudono in sordina.

Vanno su sedie a ruote i mutilati,
li accompagnano cani dagli orecchi
lunghi, bimbi in silenzio o vecchi. (Forse
domani tutto parrà un sogno.)
                          E vieni
tu pure voce prigioniera, sciolta
anima ch'è smarrita,
voce di sangue, persa e restituita
alla mia sera.

Come lucente muove sui suoi spicchi
la porta di un albergo
—risponde un'altra e le rivolge un raggio—
m'agita un carosello che travolge
tutto dentro il suo giro; ed io in ascolto
("mia patria!") riconosco il tuo respiro,
anch'io mi levo e il giorno è troppo folto.

Eastbourne

"God save the king!" the trumpets' fanfare
blares from a pavilion perched on stilts
which the rising tide breaks through
to destroy damp
horse tracks printed in the sand
along the shore.

Cold, a wind assails me
but a gleam kindles the windowpanes
and the cliff's white mica
glitters back.

Bank Holiday . . . It brings back the long
inching sea tide
of my life, too good on the rise.
Getting late. The blaring thins away,
closes in silence.

The invalids in wheelchairs leave,
accompanied by dogs with floppy
ears, silent children, or the old. (Maybe
tomorrow all this will seem a dream.)
                                     And you come,
even you, imprisoned voice, liberated
soul, gone astray,
voice of blood, lost and restored
to my twilight.

Like the door of a hotel, shining
as it spins on its pivot—
panel to panel, reflecting the gleam—
so a carousel that pulls everything inside its circle
pulls at me; and as I listen
("My country!"), I recognize your breathing,
I rise too, and the day is too thick around me.

Tutto apparirà vano: anche la forza
che nella sua tenace ganga aggrega
i vivi e i morti, gli alberi e gli scogli
e si svolge da te, per te. La festa
non ha pietà. Rimanda
il suo scroscio la banda, si dispiega
nel primo buio una bontà senz'armi.

Vince il male . . . La ruota non s'arresta.

Anche tu lo sapevi, luce-in-tenebra.

Nella plaga che brucia, dove sei
scomparsa al primo tocco delle campane, solo
rimane l'acre tizzo che già fu
Bank Holiday.

It will all seem pointless—even the power
that bonds living and dead tightly together,
fusing trees with cliffs,
and unfolds from you, for you. The holiday
is pitiless. The band
resumes its din, diffusing
in the early dusk a goodness without defense.

Evil wins . . . The wheel doesn't stop.

You knew it, even you, light-in-darkness.

On the burning sand, where you
vanished at the first pealing of the bells, nothing
but embers of the bitter brand that was
Bank Holiday.

Corrispondenze

Or che in fondo un miraggio
di vapori vacilla e si disperde,
altro annunzia, tra gli alberi, la squilla
del picchio verde.

La mano che raggiunge il sottobosco
e trapunge la trama
del cuore con le punte dello strame,
è quella che matura incubi d'oro
a specchio delle gore
quando il carro sonoro
di Bassareo riporta folli mùgoli
di arieti sulle toppe arse dei colli.

Torni anche tu, pastora senza greggi,
e siedi sul mio sasso?
Ti riconosco; ma non so che leggi
oltre i voli che svariano sul passo.
Lo chiedo invano al piano dove una bruma
èsita tra baleni e spari su sparsi tetti,
alla febbre nascosta dei diretti
nella costa che fuma.

Correspondences

Now that a mirage of vapors,
far away, wavers, then disperses,
the green woodpecker's bell-note
announces a new thing.

The hand reaching through the underbrush
to pierce with sharp tips of straw
the master pattern woven in the heart
is the same hand that ripens nightmares of gold
mirrored by the ponds
when Bassareus' chariot rumbles up
to bring the frantic bleating of the rams
back to burnt stubble on the hills.

Do you come with him too, shepherdess
without flocks, to sit on this stone of mine?
You I recognize, but what you read beyond
the flights diverging over the pass, I do not know.
I ask in vain. No answer from the pastures where,
among bursts of light and boomings on the scattered roofs,
a mist shimmers. Nothing from the latent fever
of the train crawling down the smoky coast.

Barche sulla Marna

Felicità del sùghero abbandonato
alla corrente
che stempra attorno i ponti rovesciati
e il plenilunio pallido nel sole:
barche sul fiume, agili nell'estate
e un murmure stagnante di città.
Segui coi remi il prato se il cacciatore
di farfalle vi giunge con la sua rete,
l'alberaia sul muro dove il sangue
del drago si ripete nel cinabro.

Voci sul fiume, scoppi dalle rive,
o ritmico scandire di piroghe
nel vespero che cola
tra le chiome dei noci, ma dov'è
la lenta processione di stagioni
che fu un'alba infinita e senza strade,
dov'è la lunga attesa e qual è il nome
del vuoto che ci invade.

Il sogno è questo: un vasto,
interminato giorno che rifonde
tra gli argini, quasi immobile, il suo bagliore
e ad ogni svolta il buon lavoro dell'uomo,
il domani velato che non fa orrore.
E altro ancora era il sogno, ma il suo riflesso
fermo sull'acqua in fuga, sotto il nido
del pendolino, aereo e inaccessibile,
era silenzio altissimo nel grido
concorde del meriggio ed un mattino
più lungo era la sera, il gran fermento
era grande riposo.
            Qui . . . il colore
che resiste è del topo che ha saltato
tra i giunchi o col suo spruzzo di metallo

Boats on the Marne

Bliss of cork bark abandoned
to the current
that melts around bridges upside down,
and the full moon pale in sunlight:
boats on the river, nimble, in summer
and a lazy murmur of city.
You row along the field where the butterfly
catcher comes with his net,
the thicket across the wall where the dragon's
blood repeats itself in cinnabar.

Voices from the river, cries from the banks,
or the rhythmic stroking of canoes
in the twilight filtering through
the walnut leaves, but where
is the slow parade of the seasons
which was a dawn that never ended, with no roads,
where is the long expectation, and what is the name
of the void that invades us?

The dream is this: a vast
unending day, almost motionless,
that suffuses its splendor between the banks
and at every bend the good works of man,
the veiled tomorrow that holds no horror.
And the dream was more, more, but its reflection
stilled on the racing water, under
the oriole's nest, airy, out of reach,
was one high silence in the noontime's
rhyming cry, and the evening
was a long morning, the great turmoil
great repose.
        Here . . . the color that endures
is the gray of the mouse that leapt
through the rushes or the starling, a spurt

velenoso, lo storno che sparisce
tra i fumi della riva.
                    Un altro giorno,
ripeti—o che ripeti? E dove porta
questa bocca che brùlica in un getto
solo?
     La sera è questa. Ora possiamo
scendere fino a che s'accenda l'Orsa.

(Barche sulla Marna, domenicali, in corsa
nel dì della tua festa.)

of poison metal disappearing
in mists along the bank.
                    Another day,
you were saying—what were you saying? And where
does it take us, this river mouth gathering in a single
rush?
        This is the evening. Now we can descend
downstream where the Great Bear is shining.

(Boats on the Marne, on a Sunday outing
on your birthday, floating.)

Elegia di Pico Farnese

Le pellegrine in sosta che hanno durato
tutta la notte la loro litania
s'aggiustano gli zendadi sulla testa,
spengono i fuochi, risalgono sui carri.
Nell'alba triste s'affacciano dai loro
sportelli tagliati negli usci i molli soriani
e un cane lionato s'allunga nell'umido orto
tra i frutti caduti all'ombra del melangolo.
Ieri tutto pareva un macero ma stamane
pietre di spugna ritornano alla vita
e il cupo sonno si desta nella cucina,
dal grande camino giungono lieti rumori.
Torna la salmodia appena in volute più lievi,
vento e distanza ne rompono le voci, le ricompongono.

> "Isole del santuario,
> viaggi di vascelli sospesi,
> alza il sudario,
> numera i giorni e i mesi
> che restano per finire."

Strade e scale che salgono a piramide, fitte
d'intagli, ragnateli di sasso dove s'aprono
oscurità animate dagli occhi confidenti
dei maiali, archivolti tinti di verderame,
si svolge a stento il canto dalle ombrelle dei pini,
e indugia affievolito nell'indaco che stilla
su anfratti, tagli, spicchi di muraglie.

> "Grotte dove scalfito
> luccica il Pesce, chi sa
> quale altro segno si perde,
> perché non tutta la vita
> è in questo sepolcro verde."

Oh la pigra illusione. Perché attardarsi qui
a questo amore di donne barbute, a un vano farnetico

Elegy of Pico Farnese

The women on pilgrimage, stopping over,
who chanted their litany all night long,
now adjust their sendals on their heads,
snuff their torches and climb onto the carts.
In the dawn murk the soft tabbies
poke through their little wickets cut in the doors
and a lion-colored dog sprawls in the dank orchard
among the fruitfall in the cumquat's shade.
Yesterday it all seemed compost, but this morning
spongy stones return to life,
the dark sleep wakens in the kitchen
and cheerful sounds come from the great hearth.
Barely audible, the psalmody returns in subtler spirals,
wind and distance disjoin its voices, recombine them.

> "Islands of sanctuary,
> sailings of ships suspended,
> raise the shroud,
> count the days and months
> till penance is ended."

Streets and stairs peaking in a pyramid, busy
with incisions, spiderwebs of stone
where darknesses open up, animated by the trusting eyes
of pigs, archivolts verdigris-tinted;
the song of the umbrella pines struggles to unfold,
lingers, softened by indigo dripping
over gorges, fissures, indented walls.

> "Grottoes lit by the gleam
> of the Fish carved in stone,
> who knows what other dream
> is lost here? There's more to life
> than this sepulcher of green."

Sluggish illusion! Why loiter here
in this passion of bearded women, in a raving void

che il ferraio picano quando batte l'incudine
curvo sul calor bianco da sé scaccia? Ben altro
è l'Amore—e fra gli alberi balena col tuo cruccio
e la tua frangia d'ali, messaggera accigliata!
Se urgi fino al midollo i diòsperi e nell'acque
specchi il piumaggio della tua fronte senza errore
o distruggi le nere cantafavole e vegli
al trapasso dei pochi tra orde d'uomini-capre,

    ("collane di nocciuole,
    zucchero filato a mano
    sullo spacco del masso
    miracolato che porta
    le preci in basso, parole
    di cera che stilla, parole
    che il seme del girasole
    se brilla disperde")

il tuo splendore è aperto. Ma più discreto allora
che dall'androne gelido, il teatro dell'infanzia
da anni abbandonato, dalla soffitta tetra
di vetri e di astrolabi, dopo una lunga attesa
ai balconi dell'edera, un segno ci conduce
alla radura brulla dove per noi qualcuno
tenta una festa di spari. E qui, se appare inudibile
il tuo soccorso, nell'aria prilla il piattello, si rompe
ai nostri colpi! Il giorno non chiede più di una chiave.
È mite il tempo. Il lampo delle tue vesti è sciolto
entro l'umore dell'occhio che rifrange nel suo
cristallo altri colori. Dietro di noi, calmo, ignaro
del mutamento, da lemure ormai rifatto celeste,
il fanciulletto Anacleto ricarica i fucili.

which the Pico blacksmith, hunched over the white heat,
hammering his anvil, exorcises from himself? Love
is nothing like this, it blazes with your wrath in the trees,
with the long fringe of your wings, frowning messenger!
If you swell the persimmons to ripeness, and mirror
your flawless plumage in the water, or dissolve
the fabled world of witches and wolves, if you watch over
your chosen few among the hordes of goat-men,

    ("chokers of hazel nuts,
    cotton candy hand-spun
    in the cleft of the miraculous
    rock that carries down
    the prayers, words
    of wax dripping, words
    seed-scattered by the sun-
    flower, should it shine")

your full splendor stands revealed. But less manifest now when,
out of the icy foyer, the childhood theater
abandoned for years, with its somber arch
of glass and astrolabes, after the long wait
on the ivied balconies, a sign leads us
to the barren clearing where a trapshoot
stands prepared. And here, should your soundless
succour come, the whirling disk dances in the air, then shatters
at our shots. The day demands only a key.
The weather is mild. The lightning of your robe melts
in the moisture of an eye whose crystal refracts
other colors. Behind us, calm, unaware
of his transformation, a lemur become divine,
the boy Anacletus reloads the guns.

Nuove stanze

Poi che gli ultimi fili di tabacco
al tuo gesto si spengono nel piatto
di cristallo, al soffitto lenta sale
la spirale del fumo
che gli alfieri e i cavalli degli scacchi
guardano stupefatti; e nuovi anelli
la seguono, più mobili di quelli
delle tue dita.

La morgana che in cielo liberava
torri e ponti è sparita
al primo soffio; s'apre la finestra
non vista e il fumo s'agita. Là in fondo,
altro stormo si muove: una tregenda
d'uomini che non sa questo tuo incenso,
nella scacchiera di cui puoi tu sola
comporre il senso.

Il mio dubbio d'un tempo era se forse
tu stessa ignori il giuoco che si svolge
sul quadrato e ora è nembo alle tue porte:
follìa di morte non si placa a poco
prezzo, se poco è il lampo del tuo sguardo,
ma domanda altri fuochi, oltre le fitte
cortine che per te fomenta il dio
del caso, quando assiste.

Oggi so ciò che vuoi; batte il suo fioco
tocco la Martinella ed impaura
le sagome d'avorio in una luce
spettrale di nevaio. Ma resiste
e vince il premio della solitaria
veglia chi può con te allo specchio ustorio
che accieca le pedine opporre i tuoi
occhi d'acciaio.

New Stanzas

Now, at your touch, as the last shreds
of tobacco are stubbed in the crystal
tray, a spiral of smoke
drifts idly toward the ceiling
while knights and bishops on the board
look on, amazed; and fresh rings
follow it up, more mobile than those
on your fingers.

The fata morgana that released towers
and bridges in the sky melted
with the first breeze; the unseen window
opens, the smoke stirs. There in the distance
another army's on the move—a hellish horde
of men who've never breathed that incense of yours,
on that board whose meaning can be composed
only by you.

Once I wondered whether you yourself
were unaware of the game being played
on those squares and that now lours at your door:
the frenzy of death is not so inexpensively appeased,
(is the lightning of your eyes of such small worth?),
it demands other fires, behind the thick
curtains with which the god of chance through you foments,
when he attends the scene.

Today I know what you want: the Martinella bell
tolls faintly, terrifying
the ivory shapes in their spectral light
of snow. But the man with you at his side—
he resists and wins the trophy of the solitary
vigil, his is the power to oppose
to the burning-glass that blinds the pawns
your gaze of steel.

Il ritorno

Bocca di Magra

Ecco bruma e libeccio sulle dune
sabbiose che lingueggiano
e là celato dall'incerto lembo
o alzato dal va-e-vieni delle spume
il barcaiolo Duilio che traversa
in lotta sui suoi remi; ecco il pimento
dei pini che più terso
si dilata tra pioppi e saliceti,
e pompe a vento battere le pale
e il viottolo che segue l'onde dentro
la fiumana terrosa
funghire velenoso d'ovuli; ecco
ancora quelle scale
a chiocciola, slabbrate, che s'avvitano
fin oltre la veranda
in un gelo policromo d'ogive,
eccole che t'ascoltano, le nostre vecchie scale,
e vibrano al ronzìo
allora che dal cofano tu ridésti leggera
voce di sarabanda
o quando Erinni fredde ventano angui
d'inferno e sulle rive una bufera
di strida s'allontana; ed ecco il sole
che chiude la sua corsa, che s'offusca
ai margini del canto—ecco il tuo morso
oscuro di tarantola: son pronto.

The Return

Bocca di Magra

Here are the mist and the southwester
that whisper over the dunes
and there, concealed by the ragged edge
or lofted by the to-and-fro of the breakers,
Duilio the boatman crosses,
straining at the oars; here's the sharper
allspice of the pines
diffused among poplars and willows,
and windmills flailing their arms
and the footpath that follows the waves
into the muddy creek,
moldy with amanitas; here,
still here, is the spiral
stairway, chipped rock, winding
beyond the veranda
in an icy polychrome of arches.
There it is, our old stairway, listening to you,
vibrating to the murmur
when you waken from the phonograph
a light saraband voice,
or when icy Furies blow hellish
snakes, and over the shores a storm
of screaming recedes; and here's the sun
completing his course, darkening
at the song's edges—here's your dark
tarantula bite: I'm ready.

Palio

La tua fuga non s'è dunque perduta
in un giro di trottola
al margine della strada:
la corsa che dirada
le sue spire fin qui,
nella purpurea buca
dove un tumulto d'anime saluta
le insegne di Liocorno e di Tartuca.

Il lancio dei vessilli non ti muta
nel volto; troppa vampa ha consumati
gl'indizi che scorgesti; ultimi annunzi
quest'odore di ragia e di tempesta
imminente e quel tiepido stillare
delle nubi strappate,
tardo saluto in gloria di una sorte
che sfugge anche al destino. Dalla torre
cade un suono di bronzo: la sfilata
prosegue fra tamburi che ribattono
a gloria di contrade.
                    È strano: tu
che guardi la sommossa vastità,
i mattoni incupiti, la malcerta
mongolfiera di carta che si spicca
dai fantasmi animati sul quadrante
dell'immenso orologio, l'arpeggiante
volteggio degli sciami e lo stupore
che invade la conchiglia
del Campo, tu ritieni
tra le dita il sigillo imperioso
ch'io credevo smarrito
e la luce di prima si diffonde
sulle teste e le sbianca dei suoi gigli.

Torna un'eco di là: "c'era una volta . . ."
(rammenta la preghiera che dal buio
ti giunse una mattina)

Palio

So your flight was not for nothing after all,
like a top spinning
to the street edge:
this racetrack whose spirals
here coil in,
this purple pit
where a tumult of souls salutes
the banners of Unicorn and Tortoise.

Your features don't change at the hurling
of the banners; too much flame has seared away
the signs that you discerned; last omens,
this reek of turpentine and menacing
storm, and that tepid drizzle
out of savaged clouds,
a late salute to the glory of a fate
even destiny cannot contain. From the tower falls
a clangor of brass: the procession
makes its way while the drums boom out
the glory of the districts.
                              Strange: you
who contemplate this agitated vastness,
the blackened bricks, the trembling
mongolfier of paper showered down
by moving phantoms on the huge clock's
quadrant, the arpeggio flurry
of the swarming crowd and the stupor
that invades the snail shell
of the Campo—your fingers hold
the imperious seal
I had thought lost
and the light that used to be now strews
its lilies over the blanched heads.

An echo of those days: "Once upon a time . . ."
(brings back the prayer that out of a morning's darkness
ascended to you)

"non un reame, ma l'esile
traccia di filigrana
che senza lasciarvi segno
i nostri passi sfioravano.

Sotto la volta diaccia
grava ora un sonno di sasso,
la voce dalla cantina
nessuno ascolta, o sei te.

La sbarra in croce non scande
la luce per chi s'è smarrito,
la morte non ha altra voce
di quella che spande la vita,"

ma un'altra voce qui fuga l'orrore
del prigione e per lei quel ritornello
non vale il ghirigoro d'aste avvolte
(Oca e Giraffa) che s'incrociano alte
e ricadono in fiamme. Geme il palco
al passaggio dei brocchi salutati
da un urlo solo. È un volo! E tu dimentica!
Dimentica la morte
toto caelo raggiunta e l'ergotante
balbuzie dei dannati! C'era il giorno
dei viventi, lo vedi, e pare immobile
nell'acqua del rubino che si popola
di immagini. Il presente s'allontana
ed il traguardo è là: fuor della selva
dei gonfaloni, su lo scampanìo
del cielo irrefrenato, oltre lo sguardo
dell'uomo—e tu lo fissi. Così alzati,
finché spunti la trottola il suo perno
ma il solco resti inciso. Poi, nient'altro.

"no kingdom but the fine
trace of filigree
which our footsteps brushed
and left no sign.

Under the icy vault
a sleep of stone weighs down,
no one hears the voice
from the cellar—or only you.

The crossbar says nothing
to the man who's lost the light.
Death's only voice
is the voice diffused by life,"

but, fleeing the prison horror, there comes
another voice, for which that refrain cannot compare
with the flourish of furled banners
(Goose and Giraffe) crossing overhead,
then falling back in flames. The grandstand groans
as the nags trot by, hailed
by a single shout. They're off, flying! And you're oblivious!
Oblivious to the death
toto caelo consummated and the quibbling
stutter of the damned! For living men
it was *the* day, you see it, and it seems stilled
in the water of this ruby
peopled by images. The present recedes,
and there's the finish line: there, beyond the forest
of gonfalons, high over the bells pealing
in the unbridled sky, beyond the eyesight
of man—and *you* set that line. So up, on your feet,
until the pivot of the top is blunted
but the track it cut remains. Then nothing more.

Notizie dall'Amiata

Il fuoco d'artifizio del maltempo
sarà murmure d'arnie a tarda sera.
La stanza ha travature
tarlate ed un sentore di meloni
penetra dall'assito. Le fumate
morbide che risalgono una valle
d'elfi e di funghi fino al cono diafano
della cima m'intorbidano i vetri,
e ti scrivo di qui, da questo tavolo
remoto, dalla cellula di miele
di una sfera lanciata nello spazio—
e le gabbie coperte, il focolare
dove i marroni esplodono, le vene
di salnitro e di muffa sono il quadro
dove tra poco romperai. La vita
che t'affàbula è ancora troppo breve
se ti contiene! Schiude la tua icona
il fondo luminoso. Fuori piove.

★ ★ ★

E tu seguissi le fragili architetture
annerite dal tempo e dal carbone,
i cortili quadrati che hanno nel mezzo
il pozzo profondissimo; tu seguissi
il volo infagottato degli uccelli
notturni e in fondo al borro l'alluccioliò
della Galassia, la fascia d'ogni tormento.
Ma il passo che risuona a lungo nell'oscuro
è di chi va solitario e altro non vede
che questo cadere di archi, di ombre e di pieghe.
Le stelle hanno trapunti troppo sottili,
l'occhio del campanile è fermo sulle due ore,
i rampicanti anch'essi sono un'ascesa
di tenebre ed il loro profumo duole amaro.
Ritorna domani più freddo, vento del nord,
spezza le antiche mani dell'arenaria,

News from Amiata

The bad weather's fireworks
will be a murmur of beehives late tonight.
Worms have gnawed the rafters of the room,
and a smell of melons
pushes up from the floorboards. The soft
puffs of smoke that climb a valley
of elves and mushrooms up to the peak's transparent
cone cloud my windowpanes,
and yet I write to you from this place, this faraway
table, from the honeycomb cell
of a globe launched in space—
and the covered cages, this hearth
where chestnuts explode, these veins
of saltpeter and mold are the frame through which
you soon will break. The life
that fables you is still too brief
if it contains you! Your icon reveals
the luminous background. Outside, the rain.

★ ★ ★

And should you follow the fragile architectures
blackened by time and soot,
the courtyards at whose center stands
the deepest well; should you follow
the shrouded flight of the nocturnal
birds and, at the bottom of the ravine the flickering light
of the galaxy, the swaddling bands of every anguish . . .
But the footstep that echoes so long in the darkness
is that of the solitary walker who sees nothing
but this falling of arches, shadows, folds.
The stars are much too subtly woven,
the belltower's eye has stopped at two,
even the climbing vines are a mounting
of shadows, their fragrance a bitterness that hurts.
Come back, north wind, come colder tomorrow,
break the sandstone's ancient hands,

sconvolgi i libri d'ore nei solai,
e tutto sia lente tranquilla, dominio, prigione
del senso che non dispera! Ritorna più forte
vento di settentrione che rendi care
le catene e suggelli le spore del possibile!
Son troppo strette le strade, gli asini neri
che zoccolano in fila dànno scintille,
dal picco nascosto rispondono vampate di magnesio.
Oh il gocciolìo che scende a rilento
dalle casipole buie, il tempo fatto acqua,
il lungo colloquio coi poveri morti, la cenere, il vento,
il vento che tarda, la morte, la morte che vive!

★ ★ ★

Questa rissa cristiana che non ha
se non parole d'ombra e di lamento
che ti porta di me? Meno di quanto
t'ha rapito la gora che s'interra
dolce nella sua chiusa di cemento.
Una ruota di mola, un vecchio tronco,
confini ultimi al mondo. Si disfà
un cumulo di strame: e tardi usciti
a unire la mia veglia al tuo profondo
sonno che li riceve, i porcospini
s'abbeverano a un filo di pietà.

scatter the books of hours in the attic,
and let all be a quiet lens, dominion, a prison cell
of sense that doesn't despair! Come back stronger,
wind from the north, wind that makes us love
our chains and seals the spores of the possible!
The alleys are too narrow, the file of black asses,
whose heels clatter, strike sparks;
from the unseen peak magnesium flashes answer.
Oh, the trickling that cautiously drips down
from the dark huts, time turned to water,
the long colloquy with the wretched dead, ashes, wind,
wind that holds back, death, the death that lives!

★ ★ ★

This Christian wrangle which has nothing
but words of shadow and grief—
what of me does it bring you? Less
than the marsh, softly silting
behind its dam of cement, has stolen from you.
A mill wheel, the trunk of a tree,
the world's last frontiers. A tangled pile
of straw falls apart: poking out at night
to bind my vigil with that deep sleep of yours
that takes them in, porcupines
slake their thirst at a trickle of compassion.

Notes and Commentary

The making of notes and commentaries, like translations, should ideally be a cooperative, not competitive, enterprise. If the commentary of others cannot be significantly bettered; if it reveals what is important and also inaccessible to the general reader, above all the reader without Italian; if it enhances the reader's understanding of a writer as tradition-saturated and difficult as Montale (despite his persistent disclaimer), then it deserves to be acknowledged, not raided and rephrased. I have made generous use of the work of those commentators who have significantly improved my understanding of these poems, above all the following:

G. Almansi and B. Merry: *Evgenio Montale / The Private Language of Poetry* (Edinburgh: Edinburgh Univ. Press, 1977)

Glauco Cambon: *Eugenio Montale's Poetry: A Dream in Reason's Presence* (Princeton: Princeton Univ. Press, 1982)

Joseph Cary: *Three Modern Italian Poets: Saba, Ungaretti, Montale* (New York: New York Univ. Press, 1969)

Claire Huffman: *Eugenio Montale and The Occasions of Poetry* (Princeton: Princeton Univ. Press, 1983)

Rebecca West: *Eugenio Montale, Poet on the Edge* (Cambridge, Ma.: Harvard Univ. Press, 1981)

Like all translators of Montale, I am greatly indebted to the superb collection of all of Montale's poetry, Eugenio Montale: *L'opera in versi,* edited by Rosanna Bettarini and Gianfranco Contini (Turin: Einaudi Editore, 1980), and to Patrice Angelini, Montale's French translator. And I am of course indebted to the many Italian critics and commentators who have shed so much light on Montale's poetry and poetics: Gianfranco Contini, Angelo Jacomuzzi, Gilberto Lonardi, D'Arco Silvio Avalle, Silvio Ramat, and others. And, finally, for guidance to proper understanding of "Elegia di Pico Farnese" and Montale's own poetic biography, to Luciano Rebay's "I diàspori di Montale" (*Italica* 46, Spring 1969, 33–53).

These notes are not intended to be comprehensive. Dates of individual poems have been provided so those interested may work out the unfolding character of a book deliberately arranged in nonchronological order. Poems that in my judgment needed little or no commentary have received little or none. Allusions or references which the Anglo-American reader might conceivably not recognize have been, wherever possible, glossed. Extensive commentary has been reserved for those poems that seemed exceptionally important in their own right or that shed light on Montale's structural techniques, his repertory of themes, or poetics.

Montale's own notes and self-commentary are indicated by the use of the initials *E.M.* at the beginning of each entry. (Unless otherwise indicated, the letters cited are provided in the Notes to the Bettarini–Contini edition of Montale's poetry cited earlier.) To the third (Mondadori) edition of *Le occasioni* Montale appended the following preface:

> The present volume contains almost all the poetry I wrote after 1928, the year in which the second, expanded version of *Ossi di seppia [Cuttlefish Bones]* appeared; and it is in this sense that the demarcation 1928–39 should be understood. Actually, two lyrics in *Le occasioni [The Occasions]* go back to 1926 ["Old Verses" and the first section of "Dora Markus"], and two of the four poems added to the second edition belong to the early months of 1940. In the following Notes [indicated by the initials *E.M.*], besides providing readers with several simpler indications of place and event, I have tried to clarify a few rare places in which excessive confidence in my subject matter may have produced something less than lucidity.

The Balcony [1933]

E.M.: "Actually, this poem is a part of the 'Motets.' It was published *in limine* for its dedicatory value." The poem, that is, has been taken from its original context and placed at the beginning, both as a fuller dedication to I.B. [Irma Brandeis], and as a thematic "hint," and even a further key for the reader (if he should happen to need it).

I.

Old Verses [1926]

"Old," not merely because the poem was written in 1926 and uses the landscape and themes of *Cuttlefish Bones,* but because the meter is hendecasyllabics, that of much traditional Italian verse. In the words of M.'s French translator, Angelini (Eugenio Montale, *Poésies, II / Les Occasions* (1928–39), trans. Patrice Angelini et al.; Paris: Gallimard, 1966):

> The omnipresence of the sea, the Ligurian seascape dear to the poet of *Cuttlefish Bones* (Vernazza, Corniglia, the Tino cliff, views of the family house at Monterosso on the Eastern Riviera), the theme of childhood and, up to the pessimism of the final stanza—everything recalls the first volume. But observe the differences: the shrewdly meditated rhythm, a somewhat classicizing monotony, a certain exterior quality in the details . . . a tenderness toward family memories unknown to the poet of *Cuttlefish Bones* . . . which anticipate the poems of *The Storm and Other Things*: "To My Mother," "The Ark," "Voice That Came with the Coots," "Where the Tennis Court

Used to Be . . ."—a tenderness that diminishes until the closing pessimism—all this tells us that, for the poet of *The Occasions,* the present tense evoked by *Cuttlefish Bones* has become a simple past tense.

Buffalo [1929]

—*Buffalo!:* E.M.: "Bicycle race track in Paris. We are present at a race of 'stayers' [i.e., a long-distance event]."
Joseph Cary (op. cit., pp. 285–6) comments admirably on the poem itself and the general technique of the Montalean "occasion":

> Here is an occasion that clearly calls for—and gets—a stage direction. It seems that "Buffalo" is the name of the *vélodrome* or arena housing six-day bicycle events at Montrouge in the Paris suburbs. *Le Six-day,* we may know from other sources—for example, expatriate Americans' memoirs of the 1920s—ranked high in the period as the last word in fashionable imports from the U.S.A. (hence the exotic name of the arena). It had its obligatory Negro jazz band, its loudspeakers and limelights, flask parties and film stars, cacophony of hot music, cheers, imprecations and the roar of the motorcycles preceding the bicyclists (or "stayers") in order to break air resistance during their periodic tries for records. And having summarily named the occasion through this title . . . Montale plunges us into a chaotic *medias res* whose lineaments literally look like Hell. The first twelve lines are an impersonal inventory of the inferno of this *dolce vita,* the milling mobs, the shouts, the violent alternation of light and shadow, smoke arising from the "burning gulf," the bright blond wood of the track, which I take to be the gleaming arc or arch, suggesting an Acheron at the side of which the giggling and hysterical damned line up. . . .
> The entranced speaker awakens and enters the poem to wrench himself from his vision and force a kind of saving return to the more tenable reality that is the arena at Montrouge. "I said to myself: Buffalo!—and the name worked": the hendecasyllable is hinged like the plot at this crucial point. For exotically American "Buffalo" is the name for a local reality or occasion and its utterance works like a charm to reestablish the possibly false but more bearable existence of race, moment, milieu. The last six lines narrate the rise back into the body and the teeming grandstands: impressions of recognizable life take over, the brutish surface symptoms (we know now) of the inferno below.
> What makes "Buffalo" a characteristically Montalean *occasione* is its nervous and sinewy speed, its immediacy, its effect of private life revealed, its dramatic thrust . . . clearly a real risk of obscurity is run. The problem . . . is simply a paucity of information, plus the poem's own self-confident speed, plus, above all, the novice reader's fear of trusting his own guesses which, after all, are directed and influenced by the poem itself. As we have seen, the risk is incurred deliberately in the name of dramatic intensity.

Keepsake [1929]

E.M.: "Throughout this poem, reduced to purely nominal existence, *flatus vocis,* are characters from the following operettas: *Fanfan la*

Tulipe, The Geisha, Surcouf, Les Cloches de Corneville, La Cigale et la Four-mie, Fatinitza, La Mascotte, Les Brigands, Il Marchese del Grillo, Le Coquin de Printemps, La Sonnette de l'Apothicaire, Mousquetaires au Couvent, La Princesse aux Dollars, La Fille de Madame Angot, Robinson Crusoe."

On which, Cary (ibid., pp. 283–84) again comments helpfully:

> [Montale's] note is wholly "musicological" in intent, and apart from alerting the poor reader to the *genre* of the *dramatis personae*, it is probably overspecialized. Certainly much more relevant is the title, "Keepsake," which points to the real stage, the memory of the past and the rosary or charm bracelet of affectionately recollected names that can magically accrue to a somewhat Proustian *temps retrouvé* for the poet Montale and whilom student of *bel canto*. The poem rehearses certain key moments in the lives of its trifling cast, but in so doing functions above all as correlative for the real emotion and vein of self-irony at that emotion experienced by the memory screening them. The pathos of this cumulative keepsake is produced by such details as the shivering grasshopper, the anguishes of Fatinitza and Tonio, the culminating pastoral melancholia of Crusoe's faithful Friday. Its concurrent countervein of ironic detachment is made up of such interruptive "stage" business—kin to Brechtian *Verfremdung*—as the "frying" reflector, the used-up puppet's limpness of Larivaudière and Pitou, the brusque pacing of the hendecasyllables *vivace* (rather than the obligatory *largo* of reminiscence), the sudden breaks and forced enjambements, the sonic playfulness of the irregular rhyming *passim* (for example, *ritorna-riflettore-percorre-torna, Fatinitza-agon-izza, Pitou-non danza più*, and so on). In short, "Keepsake" is just that: a catalogue of *moments musicales* made into hendecasyllables and kept "for luck," a fairly private and slight "charm" whose odd vivacity endows it with a geniality which, at least, is public. It stands by itself, a *cul de sac* or extreme, in the *opera* of Montale.

Lindau [1932]

—*Lindau:* Resort town on Lake Constance in Bavaria.

Bagni di Lucca [1932]

—*Bagni di Lucca:* "Hot Springs" resort eighteen miles from Lucca, frequented by both Montaigne and the Italian poet, Alfieri.

Autumn Cellars [1931]

E.M.: "The 'white horde' constitutes 'another moon effect'; a lunar horde reappears in 'Low Tide': images of light which pass by and *broutent* ['graze']."

Another Moon Effect [1932]

—*felucca:* a very narrow, extremely swift, Mediterranean sailing ship propelled by lateen sails, or oars, or both.

On the Road to Vienna [1932]

Gerti's Carnival [1928]

E.M.: (in a letter to Angelo Barile, July 6, 1932):

Gerti was, and is, a lady from Graz. Her husband was a soldier (glance at the barracks) and she saw him only on furlough. On New Year's Eve we had cast lots for a few gifts for our friends in Trieste, and for their sake we'd made use of a form of casting lots, fairly common in the North. For each person a spoonful of molten lead was dropped into a cup of cold water, and from the odd solidified shapes resulting we inferred the destiny of each. The rest (temporal regression, etc.) is clear. This poem should have remained "private"; this is the reason for its diffuseness and obscurity, unusual in me. Still, I've been told that the pathos was accessible even to "outsiders" and so was induced to publish it.

In a letter to Silvio Guarnieri (April 29, 1964) M. added further particulars:

"Gerti's Carnival": "your faraway shores" could also be the shore of Trieste where Gerti used to live, but Gerti was from Graz, in Austria. It's she who is present in the second part of "Dora Markus." . . . There's even a hiatus between Dora's unexplored life and Gerti's already lived life. The fusion of the two figures isn't perfect; halfway through ["Dora Markus"] something happened, and I don't know what.

—*Carnival:* In Italy, *Carnevale* (from Latin: "farewell to the flesh") is a holiday of festive revelry traditionally celebrated just before Lent, but in many places (and perhaps in this poem) as early as December 26 or January 7, and lasting through Shrove Tuesday.

—*fading iridescence:* a reference apparently to confetti.

For excellent commentary on this important poem, see Cambon, op. cit., pp. 35–53.

Toward Capua [1938]

—*Capua:* Campanian town north of Naples, not far from Caserta, on the Volturno River.

To Liuba, Leaving [1938]

E.M.: "*To Liuba.* Finale of an unwritten poem. Preceding matter *ad libitum.* It will be useful to know that Liuba—like Dora Markus—was Jewish."

Bibe at Ponte all'Asse [1937]

Bibe (second person singular imperative of the Latin word for "drink") is the nickname and motto of M.'s hostess. Stefano Tani informs me that the village of La Rùfina, northeast of Florence, produces a robust and unpretentious wine called, in contrast to Chianti Classico, Chianti "putto."

Dora Markus [1926–39]

E.M.: "The first section [of this poem] has remained in fragmentary state. It was published without my knowledge in 1937. At a remove of thirteen years (and the remove is felt) I provided an ending, if not a center."

In a letter to Guarnieri (April 29, 1964) M. wrote:

> I never knew Dora; I wrote that first part of the poem at the invitation of Bobi Bazlen [one of M.'s closest friends], who sent me a photograph of her legs. The "brutal faith" coincides with Gerti's withdrawal [see note on "Gerti's Carnival"] into an imaginary Carinthia. There's no condemnation of any faith, but the plain fact that for her everything is finished and she must resign herself to her destiny . . .

—*toward the invisible / shore beyond, your true fatherland:* Since Dora Markus was Jewish, she would presumably be waving in the direction of what is now Israel. But the combination of "invisible shore" with "your true fatherland" suggests at least a hint of later Montalean transcendence. In neo-Platonism and Christian mysticism the soul is persistently compared to an exile, a peregrine in the phenomenal world, who yearns to return to his transcendental home, with God or among the gods. Hence Plotinus's famous injunction: "Let us flee to our beloved fatherland."

—*Carinthia:* Southeastern Austrian province, bordering on Italy and Yugoslavia.

In the Manner of Filippo De Pisis, On Sending Him This Book [1940]

—*Filippo De Pisis:* modern Italian painter (1896–1956), whose pictorial poetics seem closely akin to the poetics of his friend M., himself a painter. "Rather than upon impression, sought by means of swift changes of light in order to arrest an appearance in a world destined to change, De Pisis depends upon his extremely mobile eye, which seizes on the flash of a motif in the air so as to arrest on canvas, through rapid strokes formed of color and line, the concealed life-flutter breathing in the object. It is a contact of instants: and the secret, mysterious nucleus of the image is seized and raised to visibility" (Giuseppe Mazzariol: *Pittura Italiana contemporanea*, Istituto Italiano d'arti grafiche, Bergamo: 1961, p. 71). M.'s image here is presumably a poetic equivalent, not a versified account, of De Pisis's pictorial poetics.

—*Lapo Gianni:* Florentine poet (1275–1328?), friend of Dante. ". . . l'Arno balsamo fino" (". . . the Arno, precious balm") is the second line of the *canzone* "Amor, eo chero mia donna in domino," which expresses the joys of love in the manner of the *dolcestilnovisti*.

In the Park at Caserta [1937]

E.M.: "With regard to the 'Mothers,' see Goethe's somewhat insufficient explanations."

M. is alluding to the famous sequence in *Faust* II, Act i (ll.6173 ff.) in which Faust and Mephistopheles descend to the realm of the "Mothers," Goethe's *matrices,* in the realm of Chaos, that pullulating void from which the Mothers (not unlike Platonic Ideas) produce forms or copies for the phenomenal world. Depending on one's viewpoint, Faust *descends* (into Chaos) or *ascends* (into the heavenly void of Being). "Can you conceive of total Void?" Mephistopheles asks Faust, to which Faust replies that this void has a smell of "witch's kitchen" about it: "Did I not learn and teach vacuity?" But Mephistopheles darkly dismisses this response. The void of the Mothers is of a different order. "But in the distant eternal void [there is] *Nothing!* Your footstep falls without a sound. And there is no solid ground wherever you stop." The Goethe sequence is, as M. acknowledges, insufficient but probably deliberately so. "The Mothers," like the Chaos from which, in the classical mind, all forms of being spring, or the (chaotic) modern void of the Copernican universe, are a mystery toward which the mind—whether rooted in the matrix of the "unraveling" monkey-puzzle tree or the quotidian world of real mothers with real kitchen-roughened knuckles—can only grope with transcendental striving. For M. generally, all divinity, aspiration, and noble striving derive from the rootedness of the soul in here-and-now, flesh-and-blood reality. So it *may* be here.

The great park at Caserta, now the playground of day-tripping Italians from Naples and Rome, is noted for its magnificent Bourbon palace built in the mid-eighteenth century.

—*monkey-puzzle tree:* An evergreen tree (*araucaria araucana*), a native of Chile, with intricately woven branches covered with spiky leaves (making it hard for monkeys to climb). In the gentle climate of Liguria, the monkey-puzzle tree is widely used for ornamental purposes.

Local Train [1938]

In Italian "local train" is *accelerato*—a train, only relatively and nominally, fast-moving. The poem itself, a progressive narrative of a train ride homeward along the Ligurian littoral, musically expresses the acceleration of the train (and the rising emotion of the remembering poet).

—*the nymph Entella:* The river "Entella" flows into the Bay of Genoa near the town of Lavagna, between Sestri Levante and Chiavari. Mentioned by Dante (*Purg.,* xix, 100–02), the allusion here is characteristic of Italian baroque personifications of pastoral landscapes, and, in M.'s context, suggests a return to a lost paradise.

II.

Motets

As a group, the "Motets" are the pivot-sequence of *The Occasions*. After them come the great "public-private" poems of the third and fourth sections. They are preceded, in the first section, by a group of poems "occasional" in the usual sense of that word; technically brilliant, often opaquely experimental, sometimes quite minor. But even minor poems like the "dedication" to De Pisis or "Bibe at Ponte all'Asse" are included because they display or allusively describe the emerging poetics of the sustained and ambitious poems of the later sections. If "Old Verses" provides a transition between the poetics and the Ligurian landscape of *Cuttlefish Bones,* it also hints at different poetics, a different subject matter confronted in a different, often more oblique but finally richer way. (For an excellent summary of the developing arc of Montale's work-in-transition from his first to his third books, see Claire Huffman, op. cit.) In subject matter, the poet can be said to have escaped the Ligurian littoral that everywhere dominates *Cuttlefish Bones,* or to have come to terms with it in a series of self-confronting "returns." Thus in the first section of *The Occasions* the poet presents himself as essentially a traveler or even a refugee. Thus he writes of Lindau, a stopover on a trip to Vienna, of Ravenna and Carinthia, of Triestine memories, and Campania. Only in the final poem, "Local Train," does the Ligurian landscape reappear, now radically altered by the poet's voyage-ripened homecoming. The earlier love poems, like the landscapes, are dispersed: addressed to several women, often overlapping, not concentrated on one, as in the "Motets." The "Motets" aim at locating as accurately and fully as possible the emotional antecedent or stimulus, the "feeling-occasion," that seeks an object or situation in which to incarnate and reveal itself.

In his remarkable essay entitled "Imaginary Interview" (*The Second Life of Art / Selected Essays of Eugenio Montale,* translated by Jonathan Galassi, New York: Ecco Press, 1928, p. 302) Montale described his arduous effort to create the poems apposite to his emerging poetics (or perhaps vice versa, to describe critically what he was beginning to write, though its seeds are already germinating in *Cuttlefish Bones*):

> Admitted that there exists a balance in art between the external and the internal, between the occasion and the work or object, it was necessary to express the object and conceal the occasion-spur. A new means, not Parnassian, of immersing the reader *in medias res,* a total absorption of one's intentions in objective results. Even here I was moved by instinct, not by a theory (Eliot's theory of the "objective correlative" did not yet exist, I believe, in 1928, when my "Arsenio" was published in *The Criterion*). In substance, I don't feel the new book contradicted the achievements of the first: it eliminated some of its impurities and tried to attack that barrier between external and internal which seemed to be insubstantial even from the epistemological point of view. Everything is internal *and* external for con-

temporary man: not that the so-called world is necessarily our representation. We live with an altered sense of time and space. In *Ossi di seppia* everything was attracted and absorbed by the fermenting sea; later I saw that, for me, the sea was everywhere, and even the classic architecture of the Tuscan hills was also in itself movement and flight. And in the new book I also continued my struggle to unearth another dimension in our weighty polysyllabic language, which seemed to me to reject an experience such as mine. I repeat that the struggle wasn't programmatic. Perhaps the unwelcome translating I was forced to do helped me. I've often cursed our language, but in it and through it I came to realize I am incurably Italian; and without regret.

In the "Motets" the poet's feelings and his poetics converge in one of the most stunning sequences of love poetry Montale (or any Italian poet since Petrarch) has written. The poems have been deliberately arranged so as to reveal their individual and sustained "wave lengths," feelings in complex intrication and constant fluctuation, rising-falling, hoping-despairing (or both simultaneously), as the beloved recedes or returns. Whether she is absent-present or present-absent, the presence is as agonizingly ecstatic as the absence is painful, blurring in memory only to return more vividly, and painfully, than before. Poetry, in short, designed to replicate if possible the rhythmical iridescence of *actual* feeling. Unlike the earlier lyrics, the feeling in these poems is utterly concentrated on the single presence of Clizia, on the "signs" that betray the presence of the poet's "angelic messenger," both "here" and yet "beyond," already beginning to emerge as the redemptive private *and* public stilnovistic *donna* of the succeeding poems. Cary (op. cit., pp. 292–95) comments:

> A very good case can be made for considering the *Mottetti* as a whole as an experience of signs, a story in which from day to day a lover seeks some signal or omen of his *donna lontana*. "Cerco il segno smarrito," as he writes in the first motet. Besides Clizia leaning toward the light from her balcony and the heraldic emblem of St. George, there are the fringe of palm leaf of motet eight, the ineffable ("rich and strange") insignia of the ninth, the two shining crosses of the nineteenth, the coin set in a lava paperweight ("Sobre el volcán la flor") of the twentieth, and last. . . . The route of the entire *Mottetti* sequence, then, beginning with its anguished sense of separation and ending with a kind of weary acceptance (". . . ma così sia": "but so be it") of Clizia's otherness, is mapped amidst some signs of her, some of his condemnation to solitude, some baffling. The last motet finds a resigned poet seated amidst souvenirs that have lost their luminous function as talismanic signs and have become merely objects with a past. The past is past.
>
> The conclusion of the phase of experience represented by the *Mottetti* by no means concludes the poet's attendance on his absent lady's signs. The witness of desperate longing in the book's third and fourth sections is less personal and exclusive, far more comprehensive, than in the first two. They involve a world and an era; her signs are not only clearer, to the poet at least, but have expanded in scope from the special case, the occult charm, to materials for universal apocalypse, "good" for everybody. Many Italians have recorded

143

their sense, at the time, of the *Occasioni* poems as a heartening and heroic testament of moral resistance to the regime and what it stood for in the years just before the outbreak of world war. At the center of this opposition stands the fabulous presence of Clizia, now no longer simple source of "Mirco's" anguish or ecstasy but, as he invokes her in "Eastbourne," *Lux-in-Tenebris,* the embodied principle of fidelity to the light, of ravaged but persisting resistance to the "dark forces of Ahriman" both within and abroad, of that selfless "daily decency" which for this poet is the seed of divinity in all men's keeping.

The epigraph ("Above the volcano, the flower") is from the *Rimas* of Gustavo Adolfo Bécquer (1836–70), one of Montale's favorite poets (see "Where the Tennis Court Used to Be . . ." in *The Storm and Other Things*).

You know: I must leave you again . . . [1934]

—*Sottoripa:* the seaside arcades of Genoa.

Many years, and one year harder still . . . [1934]

—Saint George: patron saint of Genoa (I have intruded "native" for the sake of clarity and rhythm), who tirelessly slays the Dragon of evil. Cary (ibid., p. 292) rightly observes that M. would not have described Genoa in such heraldic terms if he had not intended to allude to "the miraculous struggle against evil which is the essence of Clizia's angelicity." The vow, or rather hope, stated in the second paragraph would then indicate the poet's internalization of, and intense personal dedication to, the struggle as incarnated by Clizia.

Frost on the panes . . . [1934]

E.M.: "*Frost on the panes,* etc., contrast of life in a sanitarium ('Many years, and one year harder still . . .') and wartime life. The 'ballerina' bomb was used by our infantry in 1915 and perhaps afterward too."

Though far away, I was with you . . . [?]

E.M.: "*Though far away, I was with you* . . . etc., Cumerlotti and Anghébeni, villages in Vallarsa [in the province of Trent]." It was here, on the Trentino front, that M. served as an officer in World War I.

The most revealing account of this poem (as regards M.'s poetics, his reflections on the "obscurity" of modern verse, and his crucial relationship to "Clizia," the beloved whose presence-in-absence haunts most of the great love poems in both *The Occasions* and *The Storm and Other Things*) is M.'s own thinly disguised autobiographical sketch "Two Jackals on a Leash," available in the collection of his critical writings entitled *Sulla poesia* (edited by Giorgio Zampa, Milan: Mondadori, 1976), pp. 84–87 (here cited in its entirety in Galassi, op. cit., pp. 305–09):

Many years ago, Mirco, a noted poet who has now changed professions, wrote in his head, transcribed onto pieces of paper that he kept balled-up in his jacket pockets, and finally published a series of short poems dedicated, or rather sent by air mail (but only on the wings of the imagination), to a certain Clizia who was living about three thousand miles away. Clizia's real name wasn't Clizia at all; her model can be found in a sonnet of uncertain authorship which Dante, or someone else, sent to Giovanni Quirini; and Mirco's name isn't Mirco either; but my necessary discretion doesn't detract from the import of this note. Let it suffice to identify the typical situation of that poet, and I should say of almost every lyric poet who lives besieged by the absence/presence of a distant woman, in this case a Clizia, who had the name of the woman in the myth who was changed into a sunflower.

Mirco's little poems, which later became a series, an entirely unmysterious little autobiographical novel, were born day by day. Clizia knew nothing about them and may not even have read them until many years later; but every now and then the news of her that reached Mirco provided the impetus for a motet; and thus new epigrams were born and shot off like arrows across the seas, though the interested lady hadn't offered the pretext for them even involuntarily. Two very different cases, of which I'll give examples. Here is the first.

One day Mirco learned that Clizia's father had died. He felt her loss, and regretted even more deeply the three thousand miles which kept him distant, too distant, from her grief. And it seemed to him that all the anxieties and risks of his life up to that point had converged on a Clizia who was then unknown to him and on a meeting which would have to wait for many years. Perhaps, he said to himself, the war saved me precisely for this: for without Clizia my life would have had no meaning, no direction. He dredged up his past, saw himself again in certain contested villages in Vallarsa, at Cumerlotti, Anghébeni, under Monte Corvo; he found himself in mortal danger again, but already aided even then, unawares, by Clizia's star, by the umbrella of her sunflower.

That day Mirco sat in a cafe and wrote these lines on the margin of a newspaper, then cast them into the wind, which carried them to their destination: [Cf. the Italian text of "Though far away, I was with you . . ." p. 49].

Second and final example: One summer afternoon Mirco found himself at Modena walking in the galleries. Anxious as he was, and still absorbed in his "dominating idea," it astonished him that life could present him with so many distractions, as if painted or reflected on a screen. It was too gay a day for a man who wasn't gay. And then an old man in gold-braided livery appeared to Mirco, dragging two reluctant champagne-colored puppies on a leash, two little dogs who at first glance seemed to be neither wolfhounds nor dachshunds nor Pomeranians. Mirco approached the old man and asked him, "What kind of dogs are these?" And the old man, dry and proud, answered, "They're not dogs, they're jackals." (He spoke like a true, uneducated Southerner, then turned the corner with his pair.) Clizia loved droll animals. How amused she would have been to see them! thought Mirco. And from that day on he never read the name Modena without associating the city with his idea of Clizia and the two jackals. A strange, persistent idea. Could the two beasts have been sent by her, like an emanation? Were they an emblem, an occult signature, a *senhal*? Or were they only an hallucination, the premonitory signs of her fall, her end?

Similar things often happened; there were no more jackals, but other strange products from the grab bag of life: poodles, monkeys, owls on a trestle, minstrels. . . . And always, a healing balm entered the heart of the wound. One evening Mirco heard some lines in his head, took a pencil and a tram ticket (the only paper in his pocket) and wrote: [Cf. the first two stanzas of the motet "The hope of even seeing you . . ." p. 53].

He stopped, erased the period, and substituted a colon because he sensed the need for an example that would also be a conclusion. And he ended:

(a Modena, tra i portici,
un servo gallonato trascinava
due sciacalli al guinzaglio.)

(At Modena, among the porticoes,
a flunky in gold braid was tugging
two jackals on a leash.)

The parentheses were intended to isolate the example and suggest a different tone of voice, the jolt of an intimate and distant memory.

When the poems were published with others which were related and easier to understand, and which ought to have explained even their two least limpid sisters, great was the bafflement of the critics. And the objections of the detractors were totally out of line with the nature of the case. If the poet had perhaps abandoned himself too freely to his antecedent, his "situation," the critics demonstrated a very different, and more serious, mental torpor.

The first investigations concerned Cumerlotti and Anghébeni, which were mistaken for two characters, essential to the understanding of the text. Anghébeni, Carneade, who was he? asked one critic, now a doctor, who we hope brings a better clinical eye to his new profession. And who, asked others, was "Cumerlotti's girl"? Were the jackals hers? And what did Modena have to do with it? Why Modena and not Parma or Voghera? And the man with the jackals? Was he a servant? A publicist? And the father? How did he die and where and why?

I have touched on one aspect (and only one) of the obscurity or apparent obscurity of certain contemporary art: that which is born of an intense concentration and of a confidence, perhaps excessive, in the material being treated. Faced with this, the critics act like the visitor at an art exhibition who looks at two pictures, a still life of mushrooms, for example, or a landscape with a man walking with an open umbrella, and asks himself: What do these mushrooms cost per pound? Were they picked by the artist or bought at the market? Where is that man going? What's his name? And is that umbrella real silk or synthetic? The obscurity of the classics, not only of Dante and Petrarch but also of Foscolo and Leopardi, has been partly unraveled by the commentary of whole generations of scholars: and I don't doubt that those great writers would be flabbergasted by the exegeses of certain of their interpreters. And the obscurity of certain of the moderns will finally give way too, if there are still critics tomorrow. Then we shall all pass from darkness into light, too much light: the light the so-called aesthetic commentators cast on the mystery of poetry. There is a middle road between understanding nothing and understanding too much, a *juste milieu* which poets instinctively respect more than their critics; but on this side or that of the border there is no safety for either poetry or criticism. There is only a wasteland, too dark or too bright, where two poor jackals cannot live or cannot venture forth without being hunted down, seized, and shut behind the bars of a zoo.

For sensitive and detailed commentary on the poem, especially on the crucial role in M.'s poetry of syntactical ordering (and disordering), see Huffman (op. cit., pp. 51–72).

Goodbyes, whistles in the dark . . . [1939]

A poem of parting, akin to "The flower on the cliff's edge . . ." Clizia's father has died ("Though far away, I was with you . . .); now she leaves by train for the funeral. In the train's movement as it chugs from the station are fused the lover's complex feelings: the "litany" of prayer, the mingled anguish and devotion ("horrible, / faithful") of physical love, the "carioca beat" of life, here, as so often in M., represented as a circling dance of various national provenance.

The hope of even seeing you . . . [1937]

See commentary on "Though far away, I was with you . . . ," p. 144–47).

The attentive reader will note here, and as the series proceeds, a clear emotional *movement,* a *sequence* of feelings, not progression but rather alternation, the seesawing of hope, anguish, loyalty, and despair as Clizia recedes, departs, seems poised for return, or (most important for the first section of *The Occasions* and *The Storm and Other Things*) confers on the poet evidence of light-in-darkness, a persistent, saving presence of a selflessness that has "no eyes for any life / but that shimmering you alone can see," and which *returns* the light it sees to the darkened window of the poet's world.

The soaring-dipping white and black . . . [1938]

—*martins: chelidon urbica.* The house martin is the only European swallow with a pure white rump and underparts but elsewhere black. R. T. Peterson (*A Field Guide to the Birds of Britain and Europe,* Boston: Houghton Mifflin, 1954): "Its flight is less swooping, more fluttering than the swallow's, and it often flies higher." M., always precise in his ornithology, has chosen the house martin because of: 1) its migratory habits (it is only a *summer* visitor to Europe); 2) its fluttering flight; 3) its distinctive color. The martin, then, is an oblique image not only of the migratory Clizia but of the alternating feelings she arouses in the poet (but presumably also feels herself)—above all, hope / despair, exalta-

147

tion / dejection. She is absent but present, at least in hope. The migratory bird (in the season of the flowering elder) will, if the "sign" is rightly interpreted, infallibly return.

Here's the sign . . . [1938]

The "sign" obliquely hinted at in the previous poem here ripens into reality, becomes *visible* sign, the unmistakable evidence of the angelic, light-bringing Clizia. She is *there*, but *not* there, a strange presence the poet feels, perhaps uneasily, moving in his blood, pounding at his pulses.

The green lizard, if it darts . . . [1937]

The green lizard . . .: Cf. Dante, *Inferno*, xxv, 79–80: "Come 'l ramarro sotto la gran fersa / dei dì caníular, cangiando sepe, / folgore par se / la via attraversa. . . ." ["As the lizard, under the great flail / of the dog days, darting from hedge to hedge, seems a flash of lightning if it crosses the way. . . ."]

—*Something rich / and strange:* From Ariel's song in *The Tempest*, I, ii, 398–99.

Why do you delay? . . . [1937]

E.M., in a letter to Bobi Bazlen (May 10, 1939): "With me it *often* happens (and often *voluntarily*) that I'm ambiguous in this way, for example, in the motet of the woman who's on the point of leaving her cloud,

> At a puff the sluggish smoke leaps up,
> sheltering the 'point' [*punto*] enclosing you.

It's clear that 'the point enclosing you' [*nel punto*] has two senses: *at the moment that* and *in the place that,* both legitimate. For Landolfi this uncertainty is horrible; for me it's a richness. . . ."

The soul dispensing reels . . . [1938]

Claire Huffman (op. cit., pp. 172–74) comments perceptively on this extremely complex motet.

> It is not clear whether the poet's memory and mind are arranging images or whether they arrange themselves in such a way as to confound him or, strangely, to free him from poetic silence. . . . It seems that a woman, her "spirit" [or "soul"], or a "memory of her" arranges her own folk dances at each "season" of life, at each "corner" of the street and, we may construe, even in the mind of the poet for she "feeds herself," is "fed," and then grows even in unlikely places, especially in his reluctant desire for her. This desire is "closed" . . . and perhaps "secret," in direct contrast to her lively dances. The memory and the woman are inseparable; she is free, "everywhere" "diffusa" and her "design" . . . invades his thinking and his language. . . . The more "hidden" his emotion, the more "closed off"

he is, the more she manifests herself and the more her memory grows. Clizia's special ability is her ability to "grow" and "feed" on something, someone whose existence she may not be aware of, and to be everywhere, at any season, given any set of contingencies: "on the wires, on wings, in the wind, by chance." . . . Memory brings her back, yet seems negative, perhaps in reminding him of her distance from him. Not memory, but poetry, can approximate in a verbal pattern her ambiguous and insistent hold on him.

—*do re la sol sol . . .:* Clizia is also a singer; cf. the allusion to Delibes's "Bell Song" in *Lakmé* in the motet entitled, "Is it salt or hail that rages? . . ."

I free your forehead . . . [1940]

—*milky / heights:* The Italian (*l'alte / nebulose*) is typically ambiguous. *Nebulosa* means not only "nebula" or "star cluster" but "cloudy" in the sense of "obscure," "indistinct."

Clizia, at least in the first stanza, is the familiar angelic messenger with frowning brows; she traverses the icy remoteness of "outer space" (whether the Milky Way or North America). The remembering poet, tenderly brushing away the gathered icicles of her metaphysical, even extraterrestrial, remoteness, restores her to *this* world, where she wakens into a particular place and time (the medlar, the courtyard of the second stanza)—but then withdraws, dissolving into a ghostly presence more agonizingly present than the other shades responding to the summons of the poet's memory.

The gondola gliding . . . [1938]

E.M.: " 'sly' [*subdola*] song of the first stanza might be Dappertutto's song ["Scintille, diamant"] in the second act of *The Tales of Hoffmann;* but the theme isn't mannered. From pure invention, unfortunately, I succeed in extracting nothing."

Still another ambivalent bittersweet "memorial" of Clizia, "one evening out of thousands," with its familiar mix of spiritual and physical ("tar oil and poppies," the "sly song" rising from "coiled rope"), remembered intimacy made more painful by the knowledge of exclusion, of *pastness.* Dozing, alone in the gondola he once shared with Clizia, he is startled awake to the ecstatic possibility that she may yet be recovered, when he glimpses a fisherman on the embankment angling for eels. Memory quickens *out* of the past, *into* the present or future, rising, "a blurred tangle" that converges with the eel—an image, in its quicksilver evasiveness, of the beloved (cf. "The Eel" in *The Storm and Other Things*).

Is it salt or hail that rages? . . . [1938]

E.M.: "is it salt. . . ? etc. The underwater knell: very likely [Debussy's] *La cathédrale engloutie."* To Guarnieri [April 29, 1964], M. wrote:

" 'Is it salt . . .' which you aroused? Certainly it made a sound. The pianola of the underworld keeps the poem in the atmosphere of a hell which is also mechanical. Lakmé's aria was actually sung and it's a *hail* of vocal sounds."

At first light . . . [1939]

The first stanza is a remembrance of a train ride along the narrow strip of M.'s beloved Ligurian coast. Cf. "Local Train" and, possibly (at least for the image of imprisonment) "Goodbyes, whistles in the dark. . . ." The second stanza, with its anaphorical contrast of dawn and dusk, is set in the dark present (unlit window, the bottom station of a funicular, etc.) of the incarcerated poet (see "The Prisoner's Dream" in *The Storm and Other Things*), living on the memory or dream of Clizia whose absent-presence makes lulls in a war, truces, lightning-flash exaltations, or as here, "pauses still human."

The flower on the cliff's edge . . . [1937]

Reprise of the earlier motets, vividly characterized once again by the brightness of remembered happiness on some Alpine or Apennine plateau, and the darkened reality of the present. Physical space, mechanically represented once again, wrenches the poet from Clizia; but that separation is delicately undercut by the wistful remembrance in the last two lines of the first stanza of the *vividness* of the memory that linked them and whose very vividness hints revealingly at the hope-renewed intimacy of two individuals bonded by a shared world, a single gaiety.

First the frog . . . [1938]

Night as apocalypse. In an earlier published version of the poem the last three lines read:

> . . . a slate sky
> braces for the charge of three
> horsemen! Greet them with me.

Presumably that coda was abandoned because too overtly apocalyptic, perhaps too much a literary commonplace. Note that the imperative, "Greet them . . ." (*Salutali*), is in the second person singular, presumably addressed to Clizia rather than the reader (though why not the reader, if the reader is willing to be involved?).

Scissors, don't cut that face . . . [1937]

To Renzo Laurano in a detailed letter dealing with certain "untranslatable" elements in the poem, M. closed somewhat defensively by saying: "This correspondence of ours will show you how certain supposed obscurities arise in my work: out of excessive confidence. The source is anything but intellectual!"

Cambon's commentary (op. cit., pp. 84–85) on the poem illuminates both it and M.'s remarkably inventive (and allusive) concentration:

> A harsh autumn settles in on the world and in the soul, and the lumberman's hatchet falling on an acacia tree arouses in the speaker's mind the echo of another blow: the mutilating loss of Clizia. Her luminous visage should never set on the horizon of his otherwise dimming consciousness, to which her image alone imparts a focus and a shape. Two chance events from the auditory sphere—the clink of scissors in a domestic interior and the thud of a hatchet outside—start an associative reaction alerting the persona to ominous implications of severance or even death; the two literal blades merge into destiny's metaphoric one to remind him of separation from Clizia and of its bleak aftermath. Hence his prayer to an Atropos figure to stop its murderous scissors, or, more simply, to Time itself, which Dante personified as a ruthless gardener "going around with his shears" (*lo tempo va dintorno con le force, Par.* xvi, 9). His spiritual survival is at stake, but the blow is ineluctable, and it is no wonder that he should recognize himself in the suddenly mutilated acacia tree of stanza 2. Poems in which the persona of the other humans are symbolized as plants abound in Montale's first three books of verse, witness "Tramontana" ("North Wind"), "Scirocco" ("South Wind"), "Arsenio" in *Ossi di seppia*, "Tempi di Bellosguardo" ("Bellosguardo Times") in *Le occasioni*, "Personae separatae" ("Separated Lovers") in *La bufera e altro*. The cicada shell, likewise emblematic (in Anceschi's sense of the term), adds its funereal note to the realistic aspect of the scene.

The reed that softly sheds . . . [1937]

E.M.: "The reed that softly sheds. The little path runs along the ditch, the crossing [Italian *croce*] symbolizes suffering endurance; elsewhere it appears as Ezekiel's wheel [cf. "Ezekiel Saw the Wheel" in *The Storm*]."

. . . but let it be. . . . [1937]

For excellent commentary, see especially Cambon, ibid., pp. 87–89 and Cary, op. cit., p. 294 ff.

III.

Bellosguardo Times [1939]

E.M.: "I was at Bellosguardo on several occasions. The poem 'Bellosguardo Times' should have been the pendant to 'Mediterranean' [in *Cuttlefish Bones*], a sea swell, but on this occasion 'humanistic.' The surprised moment as hidden motionlessness" [*Montale commenta Montale*, edited by Lorenzo Greco, Parma, Pratiche Editrice, 1980, p. 35]. In "Intentions" (Galassi, op. cit., p. 302), Montale elaborated: "In *Cuttlefish Bones* everything was attracted and absorbed by the fermenting sea; later I saw that, for me, the sea was everywhere, and even the classic architecture of the Tuscan hills was also in itself movement and flight [*fuga*]."

In the poem's Italian title the word *tempi* could be rendered as either "times" or "rhythms" (i.e., rhythmic *tempi*), and probably is meant to convey both.

On this section as a whole and its place in the overall structure of the book, Cary (op. cit., pp. 295–96) comments:

> Certainly the effect of this poem, strategically placed as it is, is quite literally to "elevate" the point of view at least as high as the hill of Bellosguardo, from which can be surveyed not Florence and the [sealike undulation of the] landscape of Tuscany, but what the speaker calls the life of *tutti,* of all men "down there"

> . . . that movement which, in brief
> cycle repeats itself: sweat
> throbbing, death sweat,
> acts moments mirrored,
> always the same . . . [trans. Arrowsmith]

> lived out amidst the historic stones with their silent witness to "great images—honor, unbending love, the rules of the game, immutable fidelity." So the view involves something like a panorama of all human life, its furtive and transient gestures as well as those that seem permanent, its pathos and its grandeur. And at the poem's end, the prospect opens out to include elements of apocalypse: the storm, the *bufera* that will give title to Montale's next volume, makes its violent appearance accompanied by Biblical omens (surely the locusts are black-shirted) and supernatural connivances. . . . So the poem breaks off, ominously, to be followed by Montale's motto for section four, a citation from Shakespeare's fifth sonnet:

> Sap check'd with frost, and lusty leaves quite gone,
> Beauty o'ersnow'd and bareness every where.

> A grim prognostication certainly, which the basic mood of this section does nothing to alleviate, although the Shakespeare sonnet, beyond what is cited, is finally optimistic—the flowers' distillation as perfume ("liquid prisoner in walls of glass") can triumph over time. So too the presence of Clizia abides, even gains in splendor, through these anguished pages.

Derelict on the slope . . .

The onset of the storm, *la bufera,* which—as Fascism and the atrocities of World War II—menaces the precarious peace of the human achievement represented by the Florentine landscape—the Arno, the Boboli gardens—as surveyed from the height of Bellosguardo. The image of the storm battering the magnolias is vastly expanded in "The Storm," the prefatory poem of Montale's next book, *La bufera e altro:*

> The storm splattering the tough magnolia
> leaves, with the long rolling March thunder
> and hail . . .

—*the cradle falls:* As Rebecca West (op. cit., p. 48) notes, M. increasingly employs the word *scendere* (descend, fall, drop) in crucial contexts, usually linked to the longed-for "return" of Clizia (not unlike the "descent" of the Holy Spirit) or, as here, to the recurrent, ever-renewing movement of life itself.

—*unbending love . . . fidelity unaltering:* a glancing echo of Shakespeare's Sonnet 116:

> Let me not to the marriage of true minds
> Admit impediments: love is not love
> Which alters when it alteration finds
> Or bends with the remover to remove.

Sound of roof tiles . . .

—*the garden's / Canada poplar:* Presumably an allusion to Clizia, persistently associated with Canada. See "Rainbow" in *The Storm and Other Things.*

—*the locusts:* E.M.: "The locusts, like men, are part of this rupture, this fracture in the order of things; it's quite doubtful that they themselves are 'heavenly weavers,' but it's certain that they come from up there where the destiny of men is woven."

—*heavenly weavers:* the three Fates.

—*And tomorrow . . . .:* Aposiopesis is increasingly employed in these poems. If the destiny of men (see previous entry) is woven "up there" (from which come both the storm and Clizia), then, for *now,* this hellish interregnum, there can be no resolution, merely a suspension, a waiting for what will happen—something which poetry cannot, except by dishonesty, anticipate or resolve.

IV.

The Coastguard Station [1930]

E.M. in a letter to Alfonso Leone (June 19, 1971): "The coastguard station was destroyed when I was six. The girl in question could never have seen it; she left . . . to die, but I didn't know [of her death] until many years later. I stayed on, and I'm still staying. It's not clear who made the better choice. But in point of fact there was no choice."

The coastguard station—ancient, presumably of stone, built precariously on the edge of the beetling cliff—is an image, like M.'s rugged Ligurian coastline generally, of the fragility of human civilization founded on the tenuousness of memory fronting the elements, physical or spiritual—the relentless onslaught of the sea against the eroding cliff. Originally written in 1930, M. has purposely set the poem here, at the outset of the book's final section, in the darkening political context of 1938, carefully linking it to what precedes and what follows. The southwesters (*libeccio*) pick up the image of the storm-lashed magnolias of "Bellosguardo Times" but also anticipate the hellish Dantesque storm (*la bufera*) of *The Storm and Other Things.* In its pessimistic perseverance, the poem serves to resume and explore the meaning, both personal and historical, of the angelic Clizia, whose absent-presence dominates the "Motets" and who, throughout this section and almost all of *The Storm and Other Things,* stands for the possibility of redemption, of that gleam of light that in the opening poem, "The Balcony," fitfully illuminates the darkened room of the poet's world.

The geometrical image of the circle—whether as spinning compass, turning wheel, whirling weathervane, revolving doors, mill wheels, whirlpool—is present in M.'s poetry from the very beginning, but here takes on mostly negative aspects: meaningless repetition, recurrent despair and *noia,* an almost Nietzschean sense of *nausée,* all linked to a life grimly perceived as out of control or uncontrollable, a fatalistic mechanism, a web or trap from which one cannot break. The emphasis is clearly negative, but the negation is implicitly linked to the struggle to endure, to persist, to remain stubbornly loyal to a vision and a memory that seem to have vanished from life altogether. In the earlier poetry of *Cuttlefish Bones,* the poet's world, as in "Lazing at Noon" ("Meriggiare pallido e assorto . . ."), is perceived as enclosed by a wall or horizon, but there is always the bare possibility or hope of escape, the glimpse of a *varco* or passage, either into the sea before one or beyond the mountains at one's back. In the darker world of *The Occasions* the imagery of enclosure is grimmer, constantly adjusted to, and at times annexing, the circles (*cerchi*) of Dante's *Inferno.* To those damned to the meaningless repetitious *round* of tormented "existence" in this hell, Clizia brings the purgatorial hope of a circle-that-ascends, the spiraling upward movement of the *Purgatorio* (or Diotima's laddering Eros in the *Symposium*). The circle, like the images of merely horizontal drifting ("Boats on the Marne") on the current of life, looks ultimately to the anguished hope of a *varco,* a break in the meshes of the net, a sudden, lightninglike salvation; but it is one whose exhilaration, once the "instant of forever" passes, leaves only the sickening sense of being ever more hopelessly immured. The result is that fatalistic passivity or metaphysical ineptitude so vivid in "Arsenio" or a glimpse (as in the third stanza of "Stanzas") of the great gears of a mechanistic universe into which one is suddenly pulled as soon as the heavens open and escape seems possible. These are M.'s own pitiless "gyres"—all the more pitiless if one takes his stand, like the poet, in the ruins of the coastguard station, looking toward the sea where the "angel-savior" has vanished, trying to remember someone who, we are three times bitterly told, does not remember.

Low Tide [1932]

Clearly linked thematically to "The Coastguard Station," the poem also alludes to the imagery of the drowned man and his tangle of memories—the cemetery that turns out to be a reliquary but to which spring (as in the "unblossoming springs" that close "Gerti's Carnival") makes

154

no return. Compare, for instance, the positive note on which *Cuttlefish Bones* ("In Limine") begins:

> Rejoice: this breeze entering the orchard
> brings back the sea swell of life:
> here, where a dead tangle
> of memories sifts down,
> no garden was, only a reliquary.

Stanzas [1927–29]

Cary (op. cit., pp. 298–99):

In "Stanze" the topic is the mystery of Clizia, her provenance, the miracle she is, her paradoxical presence-in-absence. . . . The network of her nerves, fervor of her eyes, throb of her temples—to paraphrase the second stanza—all "recall" her fabulous journey from her origins, a journey described literally as a descent and incarnation. The beautiful third stanza evokes her *signs* as a play of correspondences with the unknown agency which sent her. . . . For the speaker, however, she is a fading revelation of the light ("a last corolla of light embers that does not last but flakes and falls") while he returns to his painful solitude:

> Maybe damnation
> is this wild, bitter blindness descending
> on the one who's left behind.
> [trans. Arrowsmith]

That is, for him the miracle has failed, blocked or obscured by his excruciated sense of privation.

> —I seek in vain that point from which
> the blood you're nourished by began, circles
> pushing on . . .

As so often in M., "point" [*punto*] is both spatial and temporal. Clizia's origins are, in short, otherworldly; she comes from a different continuum: she's a transcendental creature, it is lymph, not blood, that beats at her pulses and governs her complexion. That continuum is, I think, unmistakably Dantesque; in this case the context is directly centered on that key Montalean word, "circles" [*cerchi*], here manifestly paradisal. In the final cantos of the *Paradiso* Dante saw reflected in the orbs [*cerchi*] of Beatrice's eyes, the downward spiralings of the angelic spheres from that point of "light eternal," the "Love that moves the sun and the other stars:"

> un punto vidi che raggiava lume
>   acuto sì che il viso, ch'egli affoca,
>   chiuder conviensi, per lo forte acume . . .
>
> distante intorno al punto un cerchio d'igne
>   si girava sì ratto, ch'avria vinto
>   quel moto che più tosto il mondo cigne;

e questo era d'un altro circuncinto,
  e quel dal terzo, e il terzo poi dal quarto,
  dal quinto il quarto, e poi dal sesto il quinto.

Sopra seguiva il settimo . . .
[*Par.* xxviii, 16–31]

[a *point* I saw which rayed forth light / so keen needs must the vision that it flameth on / be closed because of its strong poignancy . . . / at such interval around the *point* there wheeled a circle of fire / so rapidly it had surpassed / the motion which doth swiftest gird the universe; / and this was by a second girt around / that by a third, and the third by a fourth, / by a fifth the fourth, then by a sixth the fifth. / thereafter followed the seventh . . .]

And Beatrice continues on to the ninth circle, explaininghow, as the circles approach their unifying center, "the pure spark" [*la favilla pura*], their light increases. "From that point" [*Da quel* punto], she says:

dipende il cielo, e tutta la natura.
[*ibid.,* xxviii, 41]

[depends the heaven, and all of nature]

Montale's context is Dantesque, but his situation is different. A Dantesque poet in a non-Dantesque time, no longer governed by the great light of Reason (*luce intellettual, piena d'amore*), he searches in vain for the divine source of the Love that animates Clizia and makes her a bloodless but saving presence "in this rotting swamp of foundered star." "And yet," he reminds himself, her nerves remember *something* of their origin in another, no less radiant—but immanent and carnal—divinity: Aphrodite (from Greek *aphros,* "foam") or Venus Anadyomene whose presence Clizia's closed eyes, when opened, reveal: "a blaze / concealed by a surge of angry foam." For another hint of this same Venus, see the final lines of the second stanza of "Low Tide."

In the Rain [1933]

E.M.: "Por amor de la fiebre . . ." Words of St. Teresa.
—*the whirlpool of my fate:* M.'s characteristic modulation of image. The well-known tango ("Adiós muchachos . . .") is transformed into the image of a man caught up in the *whirlpool* of eddying movement of Fate conceived of as the dance of life, praying, as it were, for that convulsive leap up (or out) of the circle from which the transcendental Clizia, her courage and migratory freedom conveyed by the image of the stork stroking for Capetown, has pointed the way. Memory here, as Huffman (op. cit., p. 103) astutely observes, is not opposed to time, but "a by-product, a remnant, a scrap, a brief consolation 'left' by the 'eddy' [*mulinello*]; it does not oppose fate but drives consciousness of it away, at least temporarily. . . . Thus, the poet can predict fate, and both pray to it and seek to oppose it by praying for, as it were, an 'accident,' a temporary grace."

156

Cape Mesco [1933]

Another of M.'s memory-haunted Ligurian landscapes, Cape Mesco is a promontory deeply pitted with huge marble quarries, where the marble barges and pile drivers are constantly at work and the seaside quiet is shattered by the sound of blasting. By juxtaposing and conflating past and present, myth and history, dream and reason (the poet's childhood and Clizia's), pastoral-idyllic and industrial (quarry-partridges, pile drivers-naiads, stonecutters-figureheads), the poem becomes itself an act, a *gesture* designed to *engage* memory and attached to the present and real, it may compel the return of the absent Clizia, so interwoven with the place, and, by so doing, realize and release its *shared* meaning. Just as the previous poem attempts a kind of prayer, so this poem aims at magically incorporating the absent Clizia by forcibly fusing her past with the poet's in a single comprehensive landscape.

Costa San Giorgio [1933]

E.M.: "A walk for a couple along the well-known Florentine hillside, and a little farther up, it could therefore have the title of 'The Walk.' Maritornes is the Maritornes of *Don Quixote,* or someone like her. It's well known that El Dorado was the myth of the golden *man* before becoming the myth of the golden *land.* Here the poor fetish is now in the hands of men and has nothing to do with the 'silent enemy' that works within. . . . The poem's been left half finished: but perhaps further development may be inconceivable. . . ."

E.M.: (In a letter to Gianfranco Contini, December 2, 1935): "Read this poetic effort of mine. . . . But think of the whole genuine background that's in it. You know the *leyenda* it refers to? It's the oldest (personal) form of that hallucination: here *doublée* with other meanings. Maybe too many. Still, it's a (desperate) religious love poem [*carme d'amore*]."

"Religious" may be putting matters too strongly or tendentiously. But the solemnity and certainly anti-Christian despair of the poem is, for all its obscurity, unmistakable. The Idol is Christ, whose "grave presence" is diffused everywhere, blotting out the light, obliterating hope, immuring the poet in his fatal prison, dooming him to a hopeless love for a Clizia whose eyes, turned exclusively heavenward, no longer illuminate the darkened room of the "puppet / felled." But it is out of this private sense of desolation and desperation that Clizia, as emblematic savior, is, Christ-like, reborn, the angelic messenger of the (Dantesque) Love with which she has merged (cf., "Rainbow" in *The Storm and Other Things*).

Summer [1935]

Still another passionately negative poem, almost Schopenhauerian in its sense of the tragic bounty of wasted nature—the "greening bushes" grazed by that strange and ominous shadow—the crossed shadow of the kestrel overhead—a glancing ornithological omen of the predatory (Christian) shadow that blights life and requires such squandering surrender of individual existence, such needless extinction of vitality.

Eastbourne [1933 and 1935]

E.M.: "Eastbourne: in Sussex. August Bank Holiday is the English *ferragosto*," the Italian August holiday season, when all Italians seem literally to vanish to the seashore or the mountains, and the cities seem abandoned to cats, tourists, and those who thrive on tourists.

In a letter to Guarnieri (May 22, 1964): *"Bank Holiday* [ll. 11 and 43]. The subject is *that ferragosto.* The long 'inching sea tide' is *that* rising water that follows low tide. 'Good on the rise' [l. 13] as my life in those years (1933), good but vulnerable. 'My country' is my fatherland, the anthem ['My country, 'tis of thee . . .']. The 'day is too thick' [l. 30] with objects and memories. The 'voice' [ll. 20 and 22] is the customary message of the absent-present one. The 'holiday is pitiless' [ll. 34–35] because it doesn't annul the emptiness, the grief, etc. 'On the [burning] sand' [l. 40], in *that* sunset. The evening falls . . ."

At Eastbourne, one would have expected to hear "God Save the King . . . ," but M. instead, thinking of the American Clizia, transposes the words accordingly.

Correspondences [1936]

"Correspondences," as in "Cape Mesco," and as the title indicates, link the natural and man-made world, the pastoral and industrial, in a network of "announcements" of "a new thing." *Something* is to happen, something *will* happen, but what? The correspondences seem, like concurrent *senhals,* to pose the question—to which Clizia, a presence like that of life returning, but her gaze turned transcendentally to those "flights diverging over the pass" (i.e., beyond the vividness of here-and-now), makes no answer. The opposites fold into each other, yet there is no transformation, no *Authebung* at a higher level—merely the concurrence of contraries whose brief, magical intersection seems so promising, but which make, to the expectant poet, nothing but the announcement of their own transient concord. What begins as *something* apparently emerging from "a mirage of vapors" peters out in the smoke of "the train crawling down the smoky coast."

—*bell-note (squilla):* this "corresponds" to the bell attached to the lead ram of the flock (l. 10) and the bell of the distant train (l. 19).

—*Bassareus:* cult title of Dionysus, whose Maenads (or Bassarids), in a lost play by Aeschylus, tore Orpheus to pieces. Bassareus' "chariot" has its modern counterpart in the distant train, just as the "mirage of vapors" of the first line is linked to the smoke of the train "crawling down the smoky coast."

Boats on the Marne [1933 and 1937]

In its lyrical *détente* and pastoral evocation of a gentler European civility, the work is a tonal and thematic pendant to "Bellosguardo Times"; each poem in its own way is troubled by a sense of imminent danger, even disaster—in one, the onset of the storm of passion and war; in the other the anxious sense of fatalistic drift exacerbated by the coming of twilight and the gathering rush of the river. Each is set in the shuddering slack of the present, the uneasy temporal interim between an ominous future and a past to which one cannot return except in fantasy and nostalgia but which persists, in its evidence of human greatness and a humane order, as the measure by which the future must be assessed. This is the "dream" against which the actual or breaking nightmare takes on a feeling of relentless fatality. So here the sense of drifting pleasantly, oars shipped, along the nineteenth-century Seine of the great Impressionist painters (those "bridges upside down," the picnic-life of a bourgeois Sunday summer outing) takes on, as the day's splendor wanes, the anxiety of frightening momentum, helplessness in the rush of a dark current now racing headlong toward that mouth where it enters the unknown ocean under the constellation of the Great Bear—the outward image of the inward void "that invades us." "Here"—and the poem suddenly breaks off in images that fail to cohere—the starling's spurt of "poison metal," the gray of the mouse (or perhaps rat) among the rushes. The continuity of the conversation fails—"what were you saying?"—as the unknown void (separation, diverging destinies, the loss of the old dream, the disappearing landmarks) suddenly confronts the two lovers. (For a remarkably parallel situation see "Two in Twilight" in *The Storm and Other Things*.)

Elegy of Pico Farnese [1939]

In a series of letters to his friend Bobi Bazlen, along with various drafts, M. commented closely on this poem, his own intentions, hesitations, revisions, etc. (with the request that his comments be passed along to his German translator, Leifhelm). The entire correspondence is contained in an appendix to Luciano Rebay's "I diàspori di Montale" (op. cit., pp. 33–53) and also in E.M., *Sulla poesia* (op. cit., pp. 93–97). What follows is an abridged translation of the more pertinent and revealing parts of that correspondence:

> Between the ingestion and digestion of a plate of *tortellini* washed down with Chianti, I wrote "The Elegy of Pico [Farnese]" with great speed, which I enclose for you. Get Tom [Landolfi—at whose house in Pico Farnese, in the province of Frosinone, the poem was written] to read it. Write me immediately what you think of the Elegy. It may be more suited to a German public than "News [from Amiata]" . . . [April 29, 1939]

> Thanks. I feared worse. But, as usual, when one goes into details, the *objective* value of those details escapes me (especially with you).

159

I don't know *how far* the differing perception of certain nuances stems from my objective shortcomings or to your physiologically different ear. Do I make myself clear? I don't know how far we feel the same way about the actual value of my verbal *impasto;* I don't know up to what point you feel that what's there is necessary and what is arbitrary. Apart from this, other difficulties in which the fault can be wholly mine, and of which I'll give you an example. In the distich 'Love . . . imperious messenger" [ll. 36–37—this in M.'s *first* draft, not his final] (which for me would be the center of the poem, the highest tonal elevation) there are elements which, subjectively, were most vital and incapable of neo-classical interpretation. . . . "Imperious" strikes me as unbeatable, ditto with "messenger." . . . In the copy I've sent you I've indicated the more apparent caesuras. Forgive me, I know you don't need them. I beg you to send them back to me with whatever query and marginal comment. I'll see to changing where I can. Note the verses that are too prosy or too classicizing. But it's my impression that the first twelve verses are perfect and only apparently descriptive. . . . [May 1, 1939]

I've touched up the Elegy considerably, and not in cold blood. Now I'd like to ask you for the *exequatur.* Don't think of this or that verse which may have gained or lost. The revisions have helped the whole of the poem. First there was that series of ultimatum or categorical imperatives that finished with the shoot . . . and a number of paddings. Now the rhythm passes more gradually from a statically descriptive beginning to a narrative and lyric movement. . . . Give [Leifhelm] this copy and not the others which I beg you to destroy. As you'll see, the *prilla* [l. 57] is also engaged for *brilla* [shines]. . . . The *balena* [blazes] and the *cruccio* [wrath] somehow link up with the *incudine* [anvil] and the *calor bianco* [white heat] (ll. 35–36). [May 5, 1939]

. . . *il teatro dell'infanzia* [theater of childhood, l. 51] is certainly ambiguous; it has both the meanings that you've uncovered. But only someone who's been at Pico can be certain that the theater is a real theater where plays are put on; those who've not been there will in any case have the suspicion, the uncertainty, the suggestion of the real theater; since theater in the sense of *milieu* (the theater of crime) would be extremely banal and with difficulty attributable to Eusebius [as M. called himself and was called by his friends].
So I'll leave the passage as it stands. With me it *often* happens (and often *voluntarily*) that I'm ambiguous in this way, for example, in the motet of the woman who's on the point of leaving her cloud ["Why do you delay? . . .],

A un soffio il pigro fumo . . .
si difende nel punto che ti chiude . . .

it's clear that *nel punto* ["the point enclosing you"] has two senses: *at the moment that* and *in the place that,* both legitimate. For Landolfi this uncertainty is horrible; for me it's a richness. Obviously, in this case the ambiguity is unconscious, spontaneous; in the case of *theater* it's a bit *recherché.* [May 10, 1939]

Elegy. If you press (or swell), etc. the fruits of the persimmon, etc. or destroy the improbable tale (in the sense of *tall stories*), etc., your splendor is *revealed* [ll. 38–50]. The icy foyer *that has been a theater* (in the two senses possible), etc. [l. 51]. The balconies *surrounded* by ivy, etc. [l. 54]. *If* [your soundless / succour] *appears:* "and here *even though* your succour appears inaudible, there's still the disk that whirls and which is in any case a worthy key to the day, the only one worthy of you." *Key* here stands for the picklock . . . as instrument for opening; but maybe (now I think of it) also a musical key would go (key of F, of G) in like sense, and even *diapason* in the sense of the small instrument that permits unison, etc. [ll. 56–58]; ignorant of his transformation? [ll. 61–62] perhaps ignorant of the celestial puff of air that makes even him a participant in the miracle.

As for the little strophes [in smaller type], it's impossible for me to provide a prose paraphrase. They are extremely generic, but not obscure. You should rewrite the same words in prose order. Lift (you) the sudarium, count (you as pilgrim) (or you who watch) the sudarium (I don't know what it is, perhaps the veil of Maya). The ships are *ex voto,* the islands cargo ports [ll. 15–19]. In the third [strophe] there are the sweets sold in sanctuary sacristies, a glance at the vulva-cleft mountain near Gaeta, glances at candles, etc. [ll. 42–49]

In the grottoes (of the islands mentioned above), there is the sign of the Fish [ll. 28–29], which I believe is one of the most ancient Christian symbols; in any case the doubt is expressed that Christian symbology (the green forest) cuts life in two and that Christ needs to be continued perhaps despite himself. If you can, even by changing everything, make a little syncretic lyric where god and phallus appear ambiguously blended; it's the sense of the Italian South. But a sense that the Poet (*sic*) approves only with many reservations [ll. 27–31]. [June 9, 1939]

—the boy Anacletus: According to Angelini, M.'s French translator, this young boy was a valet in the house of Tommaso Landolfi, where the poem was written. He was the "occasion" of this coda. But the name is symbolic as well, expressed by its double etymology. Anacletus was the name of one of the first popes of the Christian church—a fittingly unconscious presence in this poem so saturated with Christian references. The name is derived from the Greek for "called to service" and therefore may be a hint at the rebirth of Fascist militarism implied in the act of reloading the guns, so suited to the political situation in the Italy of 1939.

New Stanzas [1939]

E.M., writing to Gianfranco Contini (May 15, 1939): ". . . fallen into a trancelike state (something that rarely happens to me, since I usually write in conditions of cynical self-control), I've followed up my earlier 'Stanzas' which so delighted Gargiulo. 'Followed up,' loosely speaking. These "Stanzas," which might be given the title 'Love, Chess, and Wartime Vigil,' will be developed in a second version, and that's all, are somewhat different. They're more Florentine, more embellished, harsher; but they look good to me and I hope they seem so to you, above all on a second rereading. The 'Martinella,' as you know, is the bell in the

Palazzo Vecchio; according to Palazzeschi, it rings only to indicate 'disgrace.' *Inter nos* I've also heard it on certain occasions that you recognize. . . ."

In a letter to Guarnieri (May 22, 1964): ". . . 'another army' [l. 13], the gathering war. Clizia's last days in Florence. 'At your door' [l. 19] is extremely generic. But she was Jewish. The 'thick / curtains' [ll. 22–23] which chance can ruffle so that the worst is invisible. The 'burning-glass' [l. 30], the war, evil, etc."

Cary (op. cit., pp. 299–300) comments:

In "Nuove stanze"—composed like its predecessor in an unusual pattern of four symmetrical stanzas—all vain search and doubt are at an end. We are in a room in Florence; a bejeweled Clizia sits reigning above a chessboard whose pieces watch "stupefied" as the smoke from her cigarette ascends to the ceiling, composing not only rings but heraldic towers and bridges in the air. But this "game" is interrupted by another: a window is opened, the smoke is roiled, the *fata morgana* dispelled.

> Là in fondo,
> altro stormo si muove: una tregenda
> d'uomini che non sa questo tuo incenso,
> nella scacchiera di cui puoi tu sola
> comporre il senso.

> [There in the distance
> another army's on the move—a hellish horde
> of men who've never breathed that incense of yours,
> on that board whose meaning can be composed
> only by you.] [trans. Arrowsmith]

To the faint tolling of La Martinella (the alarm bell of the Palazzo Vecchio) two worlds are in contention: the forces of evil and "murderous folly" involving not only blackshirted militarism but racial persecution as against the heraldically rendered *via contemplationis* embodied by Clizia as she surveys the board. In stanza three the speaker recalls his little faith of one time, his doubt as to whether Clizia herself knew the terrible nature of the game, of the harrowing "fires" of passion and suffering it involved. But now, with the vision evoked by the poem, his faith is made firm:

> Oggi so ciò che vuoi; batte il suo fioco
> tocco la Martinella ed impaura
> le sagome d'avorio in una luce
> spettrale di nevaio. Ma resiste
> e vince il premio della solitaria
> veglia chi può con te allo specchio ustorio
> che accieca le pedine opporre i tuoi
> occhi d'acciaio.

> [Today I know what you want: the Martinella bell
> tolls faintly, terrifying
> the ivory shapes in their spectral light
> of snow. But the man with you at his side—
> he resists and wins the trophy of the solitary
> vigil, his is the power to oppose

to the burning-glass that blinds the pawns
your gaze of steel.] [trans. Arrowsmith]

The vigil's prize is surely one's authentic *mortal* soul. The *virtù* of
resistance resides in *coscienza,* the persisting consciousness of good
and evil. The guiding blazon is contemplative Clizia, keeper of the
faith, she who says no, who realizes the divinity of man through her
absolute commitment to human dignity, justice, and the good. Cli-
zia, as our lady of the chessboard, is the climactic sign of the *Occa-
sioni* volume, under Amor, from suffering and negation to the idea
of service and sacrifice first touched upon at the close of *Ossi di seppia*
in "Casa sul mare" and "Crisalide."

The Return [1940]

The "occasion" here is a sentimental—or perhaps "memorial"—return
to M.'s Ligurian landscape, the coastline of Lunigiana, where the river
Magra enters the sea. As Cambon observes (op. cit., pp. 195–96), the
poem is intensely private, a driving narrative of a secret tryst in a place
known only to two and haunted by memories attached to objects and
site. The lady—Clizia surely—puts a record on the phonograph—Mozart's
"Der Hölle Rache" [*The Magic Flute,* II], according to M.'s note—music
which "could not of itself justify the final squall." But song and storm
coincide in the lady's "tarantula bite"—at once the tormenting bite of
physical love and the even more painful bite of lost physical love remem-
bered. The bite also has the benefit of telling the poet that he is still alive,
not drowned or moldering in memory; hence his readiness. Love, as
often in Montale, is acutely painful; its anguish corresponds to its joys.
In the images of both spider and the storm the poem clearly recalls "Old
Verses," and the boy's nightmarish emergence from childhood into the
adult world of death, time, love, and loss. The storm image further expands
the sense of political turmoil in this section as a hell in which the memory
of past private happiness seems, in the perspective of present and future—
almost unbearable.

Palio [1939]

The "occasion" of this poem is the ancient and famous *festa del Palio,*
the great Sienese horse race held in the concave Campo every July and
August. The various districts (*contrade*) of the city, each with its emblem-
atic banners and insignia ("Unicorn and Tortoise," "Goose and Giraffe")
compete for the prize—a cloth of velvet or silk. The poem looks back to
the hellish *vélodrome* of "Buffalo," where the very word "Buffalo" func-
tions as the charm that delivers the poet from his trance among the
onlookers to a more solidly participant reality than that of his vision.
Here, pointedly, the charm is replaced by the angelic intervention of
Clizia, who brings with her the sense of redemption and knowledge of a
transcendental finish line *set by her.* The poet loses his earthly love, though
not his earthly passions, and salutes the miracle which (here, as in "Elegy

of Pico Farnese") only Clizia can accomplish and reveal to him—her solitary devotee. In a brutal and bestial time, she becomes an emblem of the courage and aspiration (however bitter the cost to him who loves her) which enable him to resist, persist, and, humanly perhaps, exist, even while as a man he despairs.

News from Amiata [1938]

E.M., writing to Guarnieri (May 22, 1964):

"News from Amiata": Any one of three or four villages in that area. Villages of a Romanesque-Christian savor, not Renaissance. Hence bestiary images or images of ancient religious feeling (the icon). Floorboards, wooden beams. The cages [l. 12], may be empty, indeed are certainly empty, but bird cages. The life that fables you, the life that makes you the subject of a fable. *Schiude la tua icona* [l. 17], the subject is the icon [not the luminous background].

The ravine, small stream of water. The books of hours, symbols of old things. Light effects from the peak [l. 42] undefined but almost artificial. The wrangle [l. 47] of body and soul. . . . A more or less perpetual state of affairs."

Cary (op. cit., p. 301) comments:

In the fourth section the mood is increasingly apocalyptic, Clizia increasingly remote and unearthly. The stage is set for the terrestrial-cosmic concerns of *La bufera e altro*. *Le occasioni* concludes with a last view from a height, transcribed in "News from Amiata" as a letter to Clizia. Amiata is an extinct volcano in southern Tuscany, at present heavily mined for mercury—a perfect set, then, for a poem bearing the bitter bad news of Italy in 1938. To write to absent Clizia is of course to make her present—the poet's writing table, the hearth where chestnuts explode, the "veins of saltpeter and mold" are details of the solitary setting "into which in a moment you will burst." The first section of this tripartite poem ends with that blessed apparition:

The life
that fables you is still too brief
if it contains you! Your icon reveals
the luminous background. Outside, the rain. [trans. Arrowsmith]

Fuori piove; once more there are premonitions of the gathering storm. The next two sections fall away from the vision of her presence into torment and despair. In what is surely an ironic reminiscence of the cosmic optimism of Shelley's "Ode to the West Wind," Montale invokes destruction:

Come back, north wind, come colder tomorrow,
break the sandstone's ancient hands,
scatter the books of hours in the attic,
and let all be a quiet lens, dominion, a prison cell
of sense that doesn't despair! Come back stronger,
wind from the north, wind that makes us love
our chains and seal the spores of the possible! [trans. Arrowsmith]

164

So the poem ends darkly amidst intimations of catastrophe—such is the news from Mount Amiata. Yet the short third section of the "Notizie" terminates with one starving image out of the prisoner's vigil—porcupines sipping from the artery of pity (*pietà*) that links him to his absent *donna*. Unobtrusively, then, the lady of the chess-board sponsors what is literally the last word in the book—*pietà*.

—*Come back, north wind:* "Ironic reminiscence," not, I think, of Shelley's cosmic optimism in the "Ode to the West Wind," as Cary suggests, but of Beatrice's zephyrlike words to Dante when she reveals her dazzling vision of the angelic cosmos (*Par.* xxviii, 79 ff.). The heaven which he sees reflected first in her eyes is then reported by her words: an infinity of sparkling lights, circle on circle, sphere on sphere, all issuing from a source ("From that point hangs heaven and all Nature . . ."; cf. note on "Stanzas") at whose center blazes the divine Truth. The film of worldliness that until now had darkened Dante's eyes is dissolved by her words, just as a cloudy sky turns clear under the breath of the (milder) north wind. Indeed, being divine, her words *are* the divine vision they describe—sparks flying up from molten iron, the angelic emanations of the Light of the World. If Dante cannot *see* the Truth except as reflected in Beatrice's eyes, he can at least *hear,* in and through her words, the music of the angelic spheres (*cerchi*) hymning the Light, the "fixed point" from which they issue.

This is the passage in question:

> Come rimane splendido e sereno
>   l'emisperio dell'aer, quando soffia
>   Borea da quella guancia ond' è più leno,
>
> per chi si purga e risolve la roffia
>   che pria turbava, sì che il ciel ne ride
>   con le bellezze d'ogni sua paroffia;
>
> così fec' io, poi che mi provide
>   la donna mia del suo risponder chiaro,
>   e, come stella in cielo, il ver si vide.
>
> E poi che le parole sue restaro,
>   non altrimenti ferro disfavilla
>   che bolle, come i cerchi sfavillaro.
>
> Lo incendio lor seguiva ogni scintilla;
>   ed eran tante, che il numero loro
>   più che il doppiar degli scacchi s'immila.
>
> Lo sentiva osannar di coro in coro
>   al punto fisso . . .

[Just as the hemisphere of air remains shining and serene when Boreas blows from his milder cheek / whereby the film that until now disturbed it is dissolved, so that the heaven laughs with the beauties of its every region; / so did I when my lady made provision to me [i.e., "saw before me"] of her clear-shining answer, and like a star in the sky, the truth was seen. / And when her words remained [i.e., "took effect], not otherwise than boiling iron shoots out sparks, did the circles sparkle. / And every spark followed their blazing, and they were so many that their number ran to thousands beyond the duplications of chess. / From choir to choir I heard them singing Hosanna . . .]

Boreas (l. 79), god of the north wind, is usually depicted as blowing with two or more cheeks. From the "milder cheek" comes the "mistral" (Italian *maestrale*), a mild sky-clearing wind out of the northwest. When Boreas blows from the other cheek, however, the wind is the dreaded *tramontana* [i.e., "over the mountains"] or Adriatic *bora* (i.e., Boreas) whose violent blasts bear down on Italy from the northeast. (For M.'s own poetic representation of these two northerly winds, see the sections entitled respectively "Tramontana" and "Mistral" in the poem "Agave on the Rocks" in *Cuttlefish Bones*.) In "Bellosguardo Times" it is the *tramontana* that batters the magnolias and poplars, that gusts throughout *La bufera* (see, for instance, "The Storm" and "The Ark"), and which Dante seems to have had in mind in the terrible gale (*la bufera infernale*) that lashes sinners in Hell.

Here the "north wind" has been invoked: 1) personally, as scourging the passions (in this case, despairing of fullfillment); 2) culturally and politically, as an image of apparently inevitable historical forces, the freezing stormwind assaulting Italy from the Nazi north (combining, no doubt, with local Fascist squalls) and destroying all tradition and civilized values; and 3) cosmologically, as the apparition of a terrible fatality at the heart of things. The element common to all three cases is the feeling of doomed "blockade." On the personal level, it is the self-imprisonment of a man no longer capable of breaking through to others, above all to *the* other; historically, it is the plight of a deeply civilized man condemned to passively watching while the new barbarians destroy everything he cherishes; humanly, it is the frustrated helplessness of being trapped in the toils of nature and necessity. Such a life is a living death. Its freedom is so constricted, its possibility of meaning and fulfillment so slight, that its possessor yearns for death. Or, if not for death, at least for the oblivion that would release him from the anguish of memory and hope. That being so, why then, *ruat caelum!* Paraphrased, the invocation to the north wind might go something like this: "Come, fatal and destructive wind, seal me forever in my solitary cell! Make me despair, compel me to recognize the impossibility of ever escaping my condition! Give me oblivion and spare me the pain of ever remembering or hoping again!"

But to desire oblivion and extinction of hope requires an agent who still remembers, still hopes. So long as desire and want exist, even if what is desired is an end to desiring itself, life exists. A "living death" is only *like* death; the death is qualified by being lived. Death, as Bakhtin observed, is pregnant with life. That this "life-death logic" is M.'s also is not, for any reader familiar with the poetry, a matter for argument. If pessimism pervades much of M.'s poetry, that pessimism is never, not even in the bleak world of "Arsenio" (*Cuttlefish Bones*), quite fatalistic. The bleakness (but also the miraculous moment) is always qualified. The qualification may be expressed by a judiciously placed "perhaps"; by the presence of contrary indications or "signs"; or by the insistent choice of metaphors (embers, ashes, brands, mud, swamp, glimmers, bubbles, etc.) which suggest latent life persisting, "toughing it out," biding its time. The poem "Hitler Spring," itself strikingly reminiscent of "News from Amiata," provides an excellent example of M.'s death-life logic. The "occasion" of the poem is a meeting in Florence between Hitler and Mussolini on a bitterly cold, indeed wintry, spring day. Death is everywhere. Suddenly, toward the end of the poem, as though so much death could not be endured, the poet exclaims, "O this wounded / Spring is still a day of feasting, if only its frost could kill / this death at last!" The thought of this life-in-death—his and everyone's—is immediately and revealingly followed by an appeal to Clizia, his redemptive angel and last resort. This in turn leads directly to the cautious hope, introduced by a characteristic "perhaps," that out of this "Hellish Halloween," may come "the breathing of a dawn that will shine / tomorrow for us all, / white light but without the wings / of terror, on the burnt-out wadis of the south." Out of death, life; out of despair, hope; the "logic" involved is at least as old as Dante.

But where, the reader might well object, are the latent affirmations in "News from Amiata"? Surely in the very fact that the north wind is so desperately desired. Why? Precisely because the "spores of the possible" are *not* sealed; because the prisoner in his cell does *not yet* love his chains; because the hermit-poet of a barbarous age cannot endure watching the daily destruction of everything he loves any more than he can endure his solitude and the endless jarring of memory and hope. So he invokes death and oblivion, hoping "beyond hope" that, once the *tramontana* has done its destructive work, the mistral—the other, milder north wind—will freshen, driving away the lightning, storm clouds, and flooding rains of the Italian winter. What the mistral meant to M. simply as the zephyr that succeeds weeks of Mediterranean bad weather, we know from stanzas of an earlier poem:

> Now the calm returns, the air
> is still; the waves chatter with the reefs.
> In gardens along the quiet coast, palm-leaves
> barely quiver.
>
> A caress skims
> the line of the sea, ruffling it
> an instant, a soft puff that breaks off, then
> slides away.
> ("Mistral" from "Agave on the Rocks," *Cuttlefish Bones*)

If, to this "natural" account of the mistral are added the metaphorical connotations of the passage from Dante, the poem begins to resonate, not only with the "ironic reminiscence" of better, happier days, but with the hope that stirs in both M. and Dante at the very moment when everything seems hopelessly lost. The poet despairs, or rather all but despairs, since the very act of writing a poem presupposes that communication is possible, that the "other," the *tu* to whom this news from Amiata is addressed, really exists. (Throughout his career, in both poetry and critical prose, M. will repeatedly ask himself and his reader whether poetry is indeed possible—a question that turns every poem into an act of faith.) But inside the need provoking the poem, there must be at least a flicker of anticipation, a hope that the poem will spark a response rooted in the need and / or compassion of the other. The "news" conveyed by this poem is cast in the form of a letter smuggled out of the death row (personal, historical, human) of the prisoner's "honeycomb cell" (one more positive "sign"). Its contents, ostensibly a meditation on his condition, are actually a veiled appeal, or rather two discrete appeals, each addressed to a different manifestation of the north wind: *tramontana* and *mistral*. The appeal to the *tramontana* is dominant; the appeal to the mistral is implicit, depending upon the sequential logic of the seasons (as in "Hitler Spring" or Shelley's "If Winter comes, can Spring be far behind?"). Though faint almost to the point of being inaudible, the hope that suffuses the second appeal is that Clizia, like Beatrice and her mistral-like words, will at last dispel the storm and speak her "clear-shining answer." As the final lines of the poem delicately suggest, even porcupines seek, and get, *pietà*.

The allusion, I suggest, is not explicit because it is encoded in the poet's appeal. That appeal, the reader should know, is addressed to a woman (the I.B. of the dedication), herself a distinguished Dante scholar, who would instantly have grasped the Dantesquely encoded message. Indeed, the poet's hope of being understood and answered is greatly enhanced if the message, like this poem, is written to the lady in "the language most her own." Beyond the bounds of the private language of the poem, we should not peer; insofar as the reader can detect the gist of the message, what is said is accessible and the privacy unprivileged.

The "reading" offered here is, I believe, consistent with the book as a whole, above all the "Motets" and the later poems, to which it provides a summative coda. M. himself later described *The Occasions* as lacking in the quality of "pedal, of deep music and contemplation." And it seems to me that the book might well be viewed as the poet's quest for that missing pedal—a quest successfully completed in the concluding poems. Unlike the lyrics of the first section, or even the "Motets," the final poems, and above all "News from Amiata," move simultaneously on the three levels noted earlier in relation to the north wind: personal, socio-historical, and universal (e.g., "the honeycomb cell / of a globe launched in space"). The storm that figures so prominently in the first poem, "Old Verses," is by comparison a fairly simple though highly suggestive intuition of the apocalyptic *bufera* to come. The violent cosmic dimensions of the later storm are not fully comprehended in the earlier one but, rather, hinted at in the child's anxiety over transience, death, and entry into the adult world. Or, in Montalean terms, the first poem functions as an anticipatory "sign" of the last poem, in which the storm is transformed into a metaphysical nightmare, a life-asserting death wish. In much the same way, metaphorical motifs and details of the earlier poems have been fused in the last poem into a dramatic revelation of the light-in-darkness imagery of the *envoi*, "The Balcony."

If the reader is additionally willing to admit the allusion to the *Paradiso* at least marginally into his experience of the poem, the concentration of image and theme become even more impressive. Thus the asses' hooves that strike sparks from the cobbles (themselves anticipated by the sparking hooves of apocalyptic horses in the motet, "First the frog . . ." and the fitful "magnesium flare" of lightning from the peak of Amiata combine into Montalean "signs," infernal "glintings" that correspond to Beatrice's divine words rising sparklike from the molten iron. And the image of Clizia, "our lady of the chessboard" whose shining gaze "blinds the pawns" in "New Stanzas," becomes even more vivid when linked to Beatrice's verbal shower of angelic sparks "beyond the multiplications of chess." Juxtapose the cloud-covered, lightning-lit peak of Amiata's extinct volcano with the contents of the talismanic shell of the final motet ("where the evening star is reflected / a painted volcano happily smokes") and what at first sight looks like merely "ironic reminiscence" of happier days is in fact only the negative aspect of the working of a complex poetic spell. The poem, I am suggesting, is a sustained charm, a *carmen,* intended, by jogging memories of shared happiness interspersed with echoes from a shared text, to compel the beloved to return, or at the very least, to respond compassionately. If the writer were not on the brink of desperation, there would be no need for a spell—no need, that is, for a poet, the ancient maker of spells from the beginning, to write poetry at all.

I realize that I may be pushing the interpretative point past tolerable limits, but it seems worth bearing in mind that M. himself vehemently declared these poems to be "Dantesque, Dantesque!" If this is so, then surely the conscientious reader, *Commedia* and *Vita Nuova* in hand, should make the imaginative effort to read them as they must have been read by the reader to whom most of them, and certainly the greatest, were addressed: Clizia.